W9-ART-082

FURNITURE MAKING
AND FINISHING

FURNITURE MAKING AND FINISHING

John Capotosto

Reston Publishing Company, Inc.
A Prentice-Hall Company
Reston, Virginia

Library of Congress Cataloging in Publication Data

Capotosto, John.
  Furniture making and finishing.

  Includes index.
  1. Furniture making. 2. Furniture finishing.
I. Title.
TT194.C36   684.1'042   79-4144
ISBN 0-8359-2236-7

© 1979 by Reston Publishing Company, Inc.
A Prentice-Hall Company
Reston, Virginia 22090

10 9 8 7 6 5 4 3 2 1

Printed in the United States of America

To my wife Constance,
whose assistance made this book possible.
Also to my sons Chris, John Jr., and Peter
and my daughter Marie,
who helped with the artwork

CONTENTS

PREFACE

Woodworking is a rewarding and creative craft. Transforming plain boards into fine furniture gives the woodworker a wonderful feeling of joy and accomplishment, whether he be home craftsman, hobbyist, student or professional cabinetmaker. The processes involved in furniture making include sawing, shaping, sanding and finishing with the aid of hand and power tools. This book describes all the basic skills and tools required; details time-saving techniques; and offers simple, attractive, and original furniture projects. The furniture projects were designed for style and appeal as well as simplicity and ease of construction.

The home craftsman and hobbyist can realize considerable savings by making his own furniture and, as his skills increase, he may find that his items are salable as well. The ultimate aim of the book is that, after the successful completion of these basic pieces, the woodworker be stimulated and encouraged to attempt designing and building his own furniture.

Thanks are given to the editors of *Mechanix Illustrated* and *Workbench* for permission to use original material the author produced for them.

FURNITURE MAKING
AND FINISHING

Chapter 1

LUMBER

Such materials as brass, plastics, chrome, and glass are employed in making furniture. However, without question, the most popular and most widely used material is wood. No other material surpasses wood in its conglomerate of desirable features: durability, strength, availability, wide selection of color and grain, ease of working with hand and power tools, and limitless finishes. Careful selection of wood is very important, since the ultimate cost and appearance of the finished piece depends on the type chosen. Wood is available in various sizes and types as solid lumber, plywood, and particleboard. All these forms are used extensively in the furniture industry and by home craftsmen everywhere.

Lumber is commonly classified as hardwood or softwood, but this classification has no bearing on the actual hardness or softness of the wood. In fact, some hardwoods are actually softer than softwoods. For example, balsa is the softest wood known, but it is classified as a hardwood. Pine is a widely used softwood, but it is harder than some woods classified as hardwoods. This classification is based on the type of tree producing the wood. Hardwoods come from broad-leaved deciduous trees which shed their leaves in the fall. Softwoods are produced by evergreen coniferous (cone-bearing) trees. Some examples of the hardwoods are ash, maple, cherry, walnut, oak, birch, and elm. Some of the better known softwoods are pine, Douglas fir, red cedar, redwood, yew, and larch. Softwoods are easier to work and easier to finish but are not as sturdy as the hardwoods.

Some woods are easily identified by such distinctive characteristics as color, odor, and grain. For example, black walnut is chocolate brown and often has purple streaks, cedar has a distinct aroma, and mahogany is reddish brown.

The style of the furniture being made plays a part in determining the type of wood to be used in construction. Some woods are easily finished while others

1

Fig. 1-1 Lumber is widely used in the home.

require special treatment. Oak, mahogany, walnut, and ash are among the open-grained woods which require filling the pores to obtain a fine finish. Some of the close-grained woods which do not require the filling operation include pine, maple, birch, poplar, and basswood.

Regardless of the type wood selected, it should be well seasoned. Seasoning adds to the stiffness and strength of the wood; both qualities are important in furniture making. Lumber is seasoned by exposing it to air for long periods or by placing it in special ovens where it is kiln dried under controlled temperature and moisture conditions. This drying removes the excess sap or moisture so the moisture content is reduced considerably, causing the wood to shrink. For furniture making, kiln-dried lumber is preferred because it will have fewer defects and stresses than air-dried lumber. Air-dried lumber has a moisture content of about 12 to 15 percent, but kiln-dried lumber has a moisture content of only 6 to 12 percent.

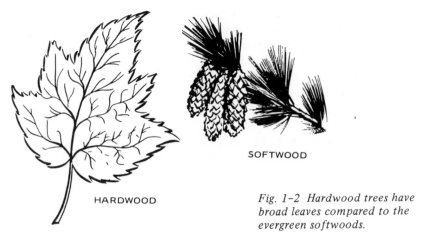

SOFTWOOD

HARDWOOD

Fig. 1-2 Hardwood trees have broad leaves compared to the evergreen softwoods.

2

Boards are cut from logs in several ways. The most common method is called plain sawing (hardwood) or flat-grained sawing (softwood). This method is faster and produces less waste. After the bark is removed, the entire log is cut into parallel slices or boards so that the annual rings form an angle of less than forty-five degrees to the face of the boards. Quarter sawing (hardwoods) or edge sawing (softwoods) is another method of cutting boards from logs. The log is first cut into quarters. Each quarter is then sawed into boards, with the saw cuts made as nearly parallel to the (medullary) wood rays as possible. The annual rings form an angle of forty-five degrees or more to the sawed surfaces. This method is more costly but produces better boards with a more attractive grain pattern. Also, boards cut this way are less likely to warp.

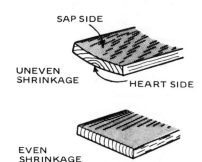

Fig. 1-3 The method of sawing a log affects its behavior in use.

DEFECTS

Fairly common defects in wood include blue stain, rot, checks, pitch pockets, and knots. Lumber should be chosen carefully, as any of these defects may detract from the appearance of the furniture piece. Knots should be avoided, except where they will enhance the piece, as in some early American furniture. If the piece is to include knotty wood, the knots should be sound and tight.

LUMBER SIZES

Lumber is seasoned in its rough or nominal size. After seasoning, it is dressed or surfaced. This is how it is sold at lumberyards. The nominal size of a piece of two-by-four lumber measures 2 inches by 4 inches before seasoning. When purchased at the lumberyard, it measures 1 1/2 by 3 1/2 inches (dressed size). Likewise, 1-inch pine, when dressed, measures 3/4 of an inch. Hardwoods with a nominal size of one inch measure 13/16 of an inch when dressed. Lengths do not vary, i.e., an 8-foot length actually measures 8 feet long. The standard thicknesses of softwoods and hardwoods are shown in Figure 1-4.

Lumber is sold by the board foot, except for moldings, dowels, two-by-fours, poles, and similar products, which are sold by the linear foot. Board-

STANDARD LUMBER SIZES			
NOMINAL SIZE	ACTUAL SIZE	NOMINAL SIZE	ACTUAL SIZE
1" x 2"	3/4" x 1-1/2"	2" x 2"	1-1/2" x 1-1/2"
1" x 3"	3/4" x 2-1/2"	2" x 3"	1-1/2" x 2-1/2"
1" x 4"	3/4" x 3-1/2"	2" x 4"	1-1/2" x 3-1/2"
1" x 5"	3/4" x 4-1/2"	2" x 6"	1-1/2" x 5-1/2"
1" x 6"	3/4" x 5-1/2"	2" x 8"	1-1/2" x 7-1/4"
1" x 8"	3/4" x 7-1/4"	2" x 10"	1-1/2" x 9-1/4"
1" x 10"	3/4" x 9-1/4"	2" x 12"	1-1/2" x 11-1/4"
1" x 12"	3/4" x 11-1/4"		
3" x 4"	2-1/2" x 3-1/2"	6" x 6"	5-1/2" x 5-1/2"
4" x 4"	3-1/2" x 3-1/2"	8" x 8"	7-1/2" x 7-1/2"
4" x 6"	3-1/2" x 5-1/2"		

Fig. 1-4 Nominal and actual lumber sizes.

foot measurement takes into consideration the volume of wood. A board foot is equivalent to a piece of wood measuring 1 inch thick and 12 inches square (144 cubic inches). A piece of wood that measures 1 inch thick by 6 inches wide by 24 inches long is also considered one board foot, as it too totals 144 cubic inches. A board 2 inches thick, 6 inches wide, and 12 inches long also equals one board foot (2 in. × 6 in. × 12 in. = 144 cu. in.). When the stock measures less than 1 inch in thickness, it is considered as 1 inch thick for calculations. Such panels as plywood, particleboard, and hardboard are measured by the square foot.

It is not unusual to pay more for a piece of wood one-half of an inch thick than for a piece three-quarters of an inch thick. The reason is that it takes more time and energy to dress down the one-inch thick wood (rough size) to one-half of an inch thick because lumber is not seasoned in thicknesses of less than one inch.

BUYING WOOD

When buying wood it is best to go to the lumberyard to personally choose the lumber. When filling phoned orders, most dealers will simply take the required number of boards from the top of the pile. Very likely those boards are warped, dirty, blemished, and defective. Boards that are cupped, bowed, or twisted should be avoided. However, it should be noted that boards which are perfectly flat at the lumberyard may warp badly when subjected to different humidity and temperature conditions at home or in the workshop. This is especially true in winter when wood is taken from a cold lumberyard into a warm, moist home.

When delivered, the lumber should be stored carefully. Boards should never be leaned against walls and should be kept off of damp floors. The boards should be checked for foreign matter. Often pebbles, which become embedded in the ends of boards, can be projected like bullets when struck by a saw blade.

Fig. 1-5 Foreign matter embedded in
ends of boards, such as these pebbles,
may be dangerous.

PLYWOOD

Plywood consists of layers of veneer—cross-banded and glued. The veneers
are thin layers of wood which may vary in thicknesses of up to one-fourth of an
inch. The number of layers or plies is always odd: three, five, seven, etc. Alternate layers are glued at right angles to each other. The grain direction of the
outer faces (front and back) are always parallel to each other. The layers directly
under the face pieces are called the cross-bands; all other inner layers are called
the core.

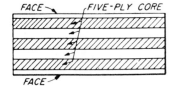

Fig. 1-6 The thickness of plywood plies may
vary, but the number is always odd.

There are two general types of plywood: veneer core and lumber core. In
veneer core plywood, the inner layers are generally as thick as the face plies.
In lumber core plywood, the center ply is thicker than the face plies. Usually
narrow strips of basswood or poplar are used as the core material.

5

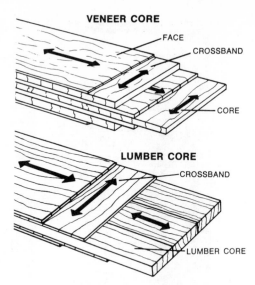

VENEER CORE

FACE

CROSSBAND

CORE

LUMBER CORE

CROSSBAND

LUMBER CORE

Fig. 1-7 A comparison of veneer and lumber core plywood.

Contrary to popular belief, a far greater percentage (90 to 95 percent) of commercially made furniture is built of plywood rather than solid wood. Pine furniture, however, is usually made of solid wood.

There are many advantages in using plywood for furniture construction. For one thing, it is equally strong in all directions, with or across the grain. It is dimensionally stable—even under adverse moisture conditions. Another desirable feature is the wide range of panel sizes available, without the need for gluing to make wide board sizes. Additionally, plywood is relatively warp-free.

Plywood is made with softwood and hardwood faces. Fir plywood is the most common of the softwood types. It is readily available at most lumberyards and is reasonably priced. However, fir plywood is seldom used for furniture, except for those parts which are to be laminated or not exposed to view, since the wild grain pattern is rather detracting.

Hardwood plywood is excellent for furniture making. Some of the woods used in hardwood plywoods are birch, black walnut, cherry, gum, mahogany, maple, and teak. If painted type furniture is to be made, an overlay plywood is available. Called medium density overlay (MDO), this plywood is made like veneer plywood, but the outer faces are made with a resin-treated fiber. The smooth surface of the MDO is an ideal base for painting. The glue used in its manufacture is waterproof, thus making it suitable for use in outdoor patio furniture.

HARDBOARD

Refined wood fibers that have been formed into sheets under heat and pressure are the components of hardboard. Made in various thicknesses and sizes, there are two basic types of hardboard: tempered and untempered. The tempered hardboard is very hard and more moisture resistant than the softer untempered type. Both are available smooth on one or both sides. Generally, in furniture making, the hardboards are used for drawer bottoms and cabinet backs. Hardboard may be cut with ordinary woodworking tools. The tempered variety, however, is very abrasive and will cause faster wear of cutting tools. The untempered type may be glued, provided the smooth surface is roughed up a bit. When nailing, special hardboard nails with small heads should be used.

PARTICLEBOARD

By combining wood chips and resin under pressure, a construction material made into sheets, called particleboard, is formed. Particleboard is made in varying thicknesses starting with one-fourth of an inch. Standard sheet sizes are four by eight feet.

Although particleboard may be painted, it is frequently used as a core stock for plastic laminates. Its smooth surface provides an excellent surface for the laminate. Because the edges are somewhat porous, edge banding is usually required.

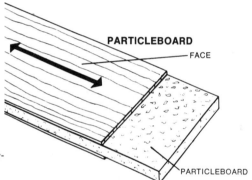

Fig. 1–8 The core of particleboard consists of resin-
impregnated wood chips.

The nail-holding power of particleboard is not very good; therefore, the use of cement-coated or annular ring nails is recommended. Nor do wood screws hold well in particleboard; therefore, sheet metal screws, with their deeper threads, should be used. Because particleboard lacks a cell structure like wood, care must be exercised when driving screws. When the screw bottoms, driving should cease. Otherwise the screw threads will strip the fibers, causing the screw to lose its holding power.

PLASTIC LAMINATES

By compressing resin-impregnated paper under high temperatures, plastic laminates are made. Hard, durable, and waterproof, laminates come in a wide range of colors and patterns. Standard sizes are available from 2 by 5 feet up to

5 by 12 feet. Thicknesses are 1/32 of an inch and 1/16 of an inch. As mentioned previously, laminates should be bonded to a core material, such as particleboard. Plywood may also be used, but the heavy grain pattern may "telegraph" or show through the laminate surface.

Nondecorative laminates are also made. Usually they are placed on the underside of the core material opposite the decorative patterned laminate to serve as a moisture barrier and to minimize warping.

Chapter 2

USING
WOODWORKING
TOOLS

Certain basic tools are needed to make furniture. Although any piece of furniture may be made entirely with hand tools, the use of various power tools makes it possible to tackle larger projects while saving much time and labor. Regardless of whether hand or power tools are used, they should be employed skillfully to obtain satisfactory results.

Hand tools may be divided into the following groups: measuring and marking, cutting, boring, and fastening.

MEASURING AND MARKING TOOLS

The rule, try square, combination square, T-bevel, and divider are examples of measuring and marking tools.

Rule

Most woodworking projects do not require extreme accuracy, but one should strive for accuracy within reason. When using a rule, it should be placed on edge when marking off measurements onto the work. This will eliminate a parallax error, and the measurements will be precise. For this reason, it is advantageous to use a steel rule with engraved graduations. The scriber point (or sharp pencil) will ride in the groove for pinpoint precision. Most workers tend to use the end of the ruler as the first mark. This may cause inaccuracies. A better practice is to measure from the one-inch mark, allowing for it accordingly by advancing all measurements one inch.

Fig. 2-1 *The rule placed on edge and marked off with a scriber will ensure accurate measurements.*

The rule may be used for dividing a board equally by placing the rule on the board diagonally with the last inch mark representing the number of divisions desired. For example, if a board is to be divided into five equal parts, the end of the ruler is placed along one edge and the five-inch mark along the opposite edge, marking off the one-inch divisions.

Fig. 2-2 *A simple way to divide a board equally.*

If the one-inch markings are inadequate—such as would be the case when dividing a four-inch board into three parts—then the two-inch instead of the one-inch divisions on the rule should be used, and the six-inch mark should be placed along one edge of the board.

Try Square

The try square is used for (1) laying out square lines perpendicular to an edge; (2) checking the squareness of an edge or end of a board; and (3) checking the squareness of the inside or outside corner of an assembly. Whenever possible, the work being checked and the square are held toward a light source. The error, if any, will show up more clearly this way. The inner edge of the handle should be free of burrs or dirt, as this will throw off its accuracy.

The working edge of the board must be true and straight before the square is used for laying out or checking. When drawing squaring lines, a sharp pencil or a knife blade is used to mark the work.

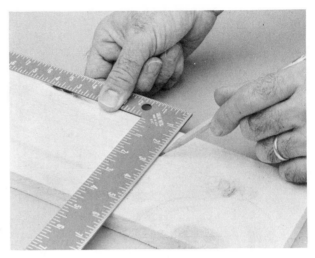

Fig. 2-3 The square is used to lay out lines perpendicular to an edge.

Combination Square

A sophisticated version of the try square, the combination square is also useful for forty-five-degree miter marking, depth gauging, and edge gauging. Some combination squares are equipped with spirit levels and scribers, and most have removable rules. A very versatile tool, the combination square may be used in many ways.

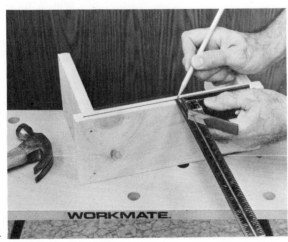

Fig. 2-4 Use of the adjustable combination square as a marking gauge.

T-Bevel

Used for laying out and transferring angular lines, the T-bevel consists of a handle, movable blade, and lock screw. This tool is not calibrated; the desired angle is set by the use of a protractor. The T-bevel may be used to "take" an angle from a cut piece and to set the tilt of a saber saw or other tool.

Fig. 2-5 Taking an angular measurement from a piece of stock.

Divider

Used for laying out arcs and circles, the divider has two steel points. Some dividers are made to take a pencil point, in which case they are called compasses. The divider is also useful for dividing a line into equal parts and for bisecting angles. For normal woodworking layouts, the pencil-point divider is sufficient. However, if very accurate layouts are required, the twin-point divider should be utilized. In use, the outboard point of the divider is manipulated to scratch a line into the wood surface of the work piece. This has two disadvantages: the surface may be damaged, and the line may be difficult to see. A better method is to insert carbon paper under the outboard point with the carbon face down on the work surface. This will result in a very fine but dark line which is easily seen and will not mar the surface.

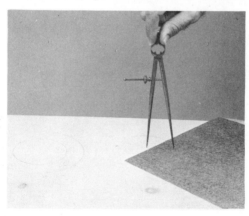

Fig. 2-6 Use of carbon paper to lay out circles on work piece.

When the size of the circle or arc is too large for the capacity of the divider, a set of trammel points must be used. Trammel points are designed to clamp to a steel bar or wood strip of convenient length. Lacking a set of trammel points, a substitute may be made by using a strip of wood and a pushpin or nail. A small notch, filed at one end of the strip, will accommodate the point of a pencil. A pin or nail is placed at the center mark, and then the trammel is used as shown in the illustration.

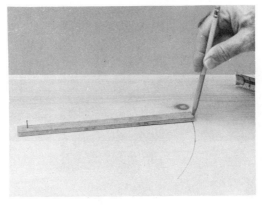

Fig. 2-7 A strip of wood pivoted at one end serves as a trammel.

CUTTING TOOLS

The main cutting tools used in making furniture consist of saws, planes, and chisels. The handsaw is seldom used in the modern homeshop, since most craftsmen today have power saws which will do the job faster and better.

Backsaw

With a reinforced metal back for rigidity, the backsaw has a thin blade and fine teeth which make it ideally suited for cutting moldings. It is also utilized in making such frame joints as the mortise and tenon. The backsaw is used in the miter box when cutting miters. If crown molding is being cut, the molding in the miter box should be supported at the same angle in which it will be mounted.

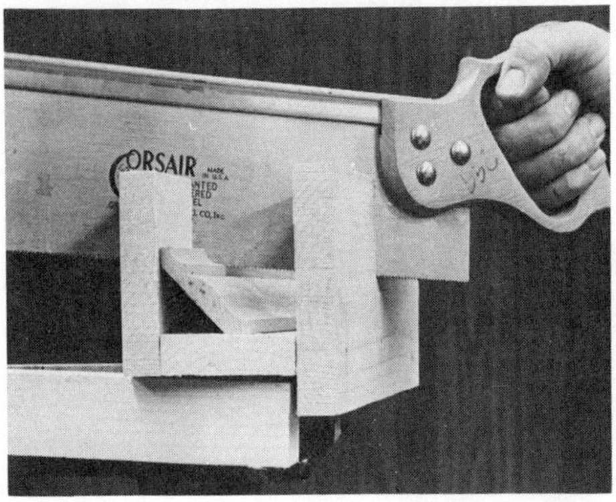

Fig. 2-8 Cutting molding in a miter box. The work is held at the mounting angle.

Coping Saw

The coping saw is used for cutting curved and irregular shapes, both internally and externally. It is also used for coping miters of moldings. When making internal cuts, a small hole is drilled in the waste area for blade entry. In normal use, the blade should be installed with the teeth pointing downward, so the cutting is done on the downstroke. If the work is held in a vise, the teeth of the blade should point away from the handle, in which case the cut will be made on the push-stroke.

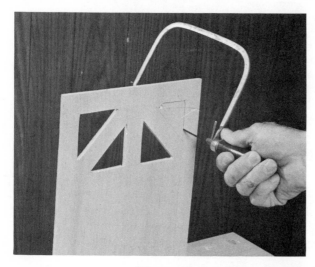

Fig. 2-9 One feature of the coping saw is its ability to make internal cutouts.

When using a delicate blade for very fine work, a little wax should be rubbed on the blade to prevent breakage.

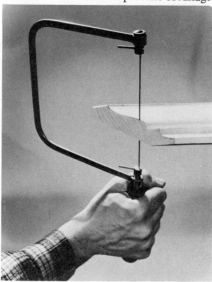

Fig. 2-10 The coping saw making a cut that gave it its name.

Planes

Planes are used for cutting and smoothing rough surfaces, for bringing work down to size, and for cutting bevels and chamfers. When truing the edge of boards, the longest plane that is practical for the job at hand should be used, since smaller planes tend to ride the "bumps."

Fig. 2-11 The block plane is well suited for truing up end grain.

The block plane, which is small and may be held in one hand, has a shallow blade angle and is excellent for planing end grain. The block plane is also used for rounding off corners of pine furniture to give it a worn look. Another useful tool for this purpose is the shaving tool, which is held in one hand and used somewhat like a rasp. The shaving tool has a curved blade which resembles a cheese grater, cuts easily, and is very versatile. The tool is also made in other shapes and sizes.

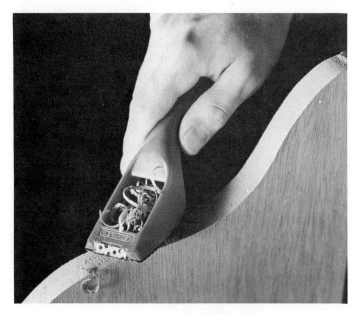

Fig. 2-12 A "cheese grater" used for shaping stock.

Chisels

Among its many uses, the chisel is ideally suited for cutting gains for hinges. For this purpose, the butt chisel is recommended.

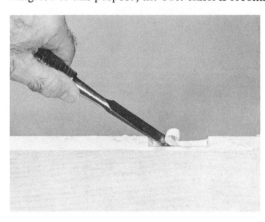

Fig. 2-13 The hand chisel is still useful for cutting gains for hinges.

BORING TOOLS

The two basic tools used for making holes in wood are the hand drill and bit brace. Generally, the hand drill is used for holes up to 11/64 inch in diameter. The hand drill resembles an egg beater and takes regular twist drills. Although it is found in some workshops, its electric counterpart has practically made the hand drill obsolete.

The bit brace is still widely used, mainly because it may be used for making very large holes—up to three inches in diameter—when fitted with an expansive bit. The bit brace may also be chucked with screwdriver tips and countersinks, thus making it quite versatile.

A popular tool in the workshop, the push drill rotates when the handle is depressed. Most are made to hold a supply of drill points in the handle. The push drill is used for making pilot holes for screws and for other small holes. When using the push drill for making screw holes for hinges, the center is marked for the hole first by using an awl; then drilling may proceed.

Fig. 2-14 Push drills are often used to bore screw pilot holes.

FASTENING TOOLS

Several tools fall into the category of fastening tools. The most common are the hammer and screwdriver. To perform quality work, quality tools must be used. The hammer is no exception. Good hammers have heads made of drop-forged steel; cheap hammers have dangerous cast heads which may break while in use. Hammer sizes are determined by the weight of the head, ranging from seven to twenty ounces. The business end or face of the hammer may be flat or bell shaped. The bell-shaped face is slightly convex and less likely to show hammer marks on the work, but it requires somewhat more precise handling than the flat-faced hammer. Actually, when making furniture it is best to hammer the nail only until the head protrudes slightly, then to drive the nail home with a nail set.

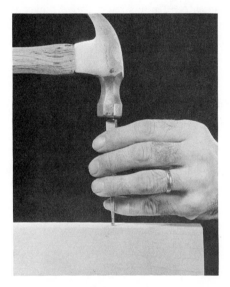

Fig. 2-15 Sinking nail heads with a nail set.

Varying in length as well as in tip size and shape, the most common screwdrivers are used for slotted and cross-slotted (Phillips) screws. To function correctly, the tip must be properly shaped and hardened and must fit the screw snugly. For slotted screws, the tip should fit the slot snugly and be no wider than the slot. The slotted screwdriver for general use has a blade which tapers slightly at the tip. When driving screws into counterbored holes, the cabinet-tip driver, which has straight sides and is less apt to tear the sides of the hole, is used.

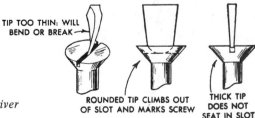

TIP TOO THIN: WILL BEND OR BREAK→

ROUNDED TIP CLIMBS OUT OF SLOT AND MARKS SCREW

THICK TIP DOES NOT SEAT IN SLOT

Fig. 2-16 Proper screwdriver tip is important.

As a safety precaution, a screw should never be held while it is being driven. A slip of the tip may cause serious finger injuries.

PORTABLE POWER TOOLS

Portable power tools are time savers. Almost any job may be performed with hand tools alone. However, in today's fast-moving society, few people have the time or patience to do hand work when power tools are so easily obtainable. Certainly there are many tasks which are best done with hand tools, but why drill, saw, or shape a piece of wood by hand when it may be done ten times faster with a power tool? Thanks to modern technology, excellent tools are available at moderate cost today. Used properly, better work is produced more efficiently. The commonly used power tools include the saw, drill, router, and sander. Power tools are classified as portable and stationary. The portable tools may be carried to the work. In most cases with stationary tools, which are usually floor- or bench-mounted, the work is carried to the tool.

Portable Saw

The size of a portable saw, also known as a circular saw, is determined by its blade size. A seven-inch saw has a blade diameter of seven inches. Normally, the blade should protrude about one-fourth of an inch below the work. The depth of the cut is adjustable by regulating the saw base, which may also be tilted for making angular cuts.

Fig. 2-17 Beveling a two-by-four with a portable saw.

Since these saws cut on the upstroke, they leave splinters on the top side of the cut. Therefore, paneling or other material where splintering matters should be cut with the good side face down.

When using a portable saw, the following safety precautions must be observed:

- The saw should never be forced through the work, as this may cause the motor to overload.
- Short pieces should never be cut on the portable saw.
- The work should be supported properly.
- The user should not stand in the line of cut.
- When changing blades, the saw should be unplugged.

Although the portable saw is not considered a precision tool, it may be quite exact if used properly. It can very well take the place of a stationary table saw. For instance, a straightedge guide may be clamped to a panel for ripping large panels.

Fig. 2–18 Used with a guide, the portable saw will make straight cuts.

The accuracy of the cut depends on how carefully the guide is set. Angular cuts may be made the same way. The work should be well supported, especially when ripping large panels. Work that is not supported properly will tend to close the kerf, which may cause the saw to kick back. A mitering guide for use with the portable saw ensures accurate forty-five-degree cuts.

Fig. 2–19 Mitering guide accessory for the portable saw. It may also be used with saber saws and routers.

Fig. 2-20 Ripping guide attaches to the base of the saw. Rip widths are limited to narrow strips.

For ripping narrow boards, a ripping guide may be fastened to the saw.

If this saw is used for rough cutting, a little waste should be cut to the outside of the line, which will permit dressing the piece to size with other tools.

Since the blade depth is adjustable on these saws, they may also be used for making dadoes, rabbets, and grooves. It should be pointed out that there are other tools more suited to make these various cuts; however, some craftsmen may not have the more specialized tools.

To make the dado, the blade is set to the required depth and guides are clamped to the work. These are positioned so the saw cuts coincide with the outer limits of the dado. Both outer cuts are made, and then the waste between is removed by making a series of overlapping cuts.

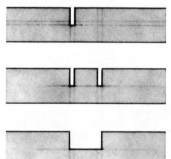

Fig. 2-21 Three steps in cutting a dado with the portable saw.

Grooves and rabbets are made in a similar manner. The difference between these cuts is in their location. The dado is a groove cut across the grain of the wood. The groove cut is made parallel to the grain. The rabbet is a similar cut along the edge of a board.

Saber Saw

Also called a jigsaw, the saber saw is used for making straight and curved cuts in various materials. The blade used is determined by the material being

Fig. 2-22 *Using the saber saw for making irregular cuts. This tool has a rotatable blade which may be operated independently of the base.*

cut. A good selection of blades for the saw should include fine and coarse and hollow-ground types. The hollow-ground blade produces a smooth cut. Like the portable circular saw, it, too, is a freehand tool but the use of guides may increase its usefulness. Some saws are equipped with a rip fence accessory which attaches to the base plate. However, the width of the cut is limited to the size

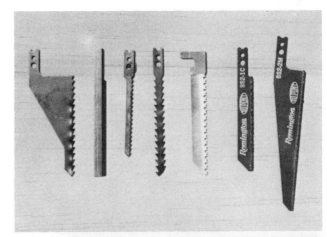

Fig. 2-23 *Various blades used with saber saws. The odd looking double-sided blade can cut in two directions, without turning the blade.*

Fig. 2-24 *Some saber saws may be fitted with a side guide for ripping operations.*

Fig. 2-25 *Another method of ripping with the saber saw utilizes a straight-edge clamped to the stock.*

of the crossbar. A board clamped to the work is more practical and perhaps more accurate. The saber saw also cuts on the upstroke, so splintering, if any, will take place on the upper side of the work. If it is not practical to cut from the back side, placing masking tape over the line of cut, then drawing the cutting line on it will provide some help. Wide blades are used for straight cutting; narrow blades produce the sharpest curves.

When using the saw freehand, the work should be supported properly to prevent excess vibration which may cause a sloppy cut. If necessary, clamps should be used.

Fig. 2-26 *Some saws have variable speed switches to accommodate various types and thicknesses of materials.*

For cutting arcs and circles, the saber saw may be fitted with a pivot guide. The size of the circles that can be cut is only limited by the length of the guide. A guide is easily made by using a suitable strip of steel.

The saber saw may be used to make pocket cuts without first making a blade entry hole by tilting the saw forward, using the front of the base as a pivot point, starting the saw, and then slowly letting the blade cut into the waste. When the base is flat against the work, cutting is started in the usual manner.

FRONT OF BLADE

PIVOT POINT

BLADE & PIVOT
MUST BE IN
LINE

Fig. 2-27 When cutting arcs and circles with the pivot guide, the pivot point must be in line with the blade.

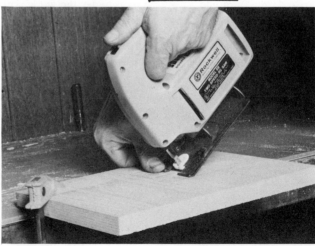

Fig. 2-28 Making a pocket cut with the saber saw.

23

Electric Drill

Designed primarily for boring holes, the electric drill may also be used to perform other duties, such as grinding, sanding, and even cutting when fitted with special accessories. Drills come in three sizes: quarter inch, three-eighths inch, and half inch. They are also made in three-quarter inch and larger, but not for home use. The size indicates the largest bit the tool will hold. However, spade bits which will bore holes greater than one inch in diameter are made with quarter-inch shanks so they can be used in any of the above drills. Other bits for countersinking, filing, and grinding are also made for the electric drill.

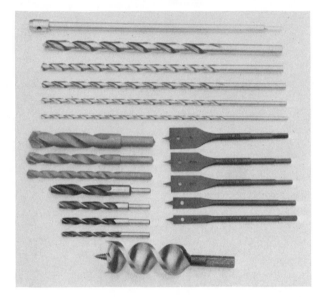

Fig. 2-29 Various drills and bits used for boring holes. The straight piece at the top is an extension.

When using the drill, to prevent splintering the hole edge, a back-up piece should always be used under the work. This is especially important when using the spade bits.

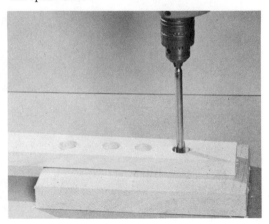

Fig. 2-30 Back-up board prevents splintering on the underside of stock.

Another important bit used with the drill is the screwmate, which makes it possible to drill in one operation the body hole, shank clearance, and countersink for screws.

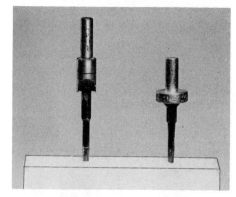

Fig. 2-31 Two types of screw pilots: the one on the left makes counterbored holes; the other is for flathead screws.

If a drill is of the variable-speed type, a low-speed setting may be used for driving screws. Special screwdriving accessories are made for this purpose.

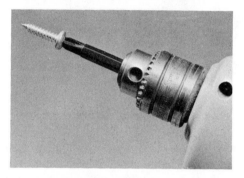

Fig. 2-32 Slow-speed drills may be fitted with screwdriver tips.

Large diameter holes are made with a hole saw. These may be used in portable or stationary drills and will make holes of up to 2-1/2 inches in diameter.

Fig. 2-33 A variety of hole saws and the mandrels which hold them.

Router

The router has limited uses, but is is one of the most important tools in the workshop. Designed primarily for shaping the edges of wood, it is also used for dadoing, rabbeting, mortising, trimming plastic laminates, with patterns or templates for making duplicate pieces, and dressing the edges of wood. Self-piloting cutters eliminate the need for guides.

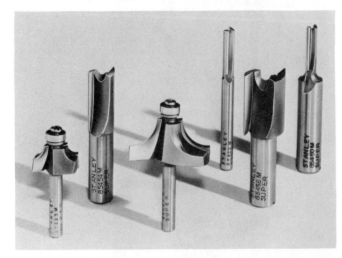

Fig. 2-34 Various router cutters. Some have ball-bearing guides.

The router motor runs at very high speeds (20,000 to 30,000 RPM). With sharp cutters it will produce an extremely fine edge which does not require sanding. The depth of the cut is adjusted by rotating a collar on the body of the machine. Very fine adjustments are thus possible.

Rabbeting is done with a rabbeting bit which is made to follow the edge of the work. The cutter is lowered to the proper depth. If the wood is hard or if the rabbet is large, several passes should be made, increasing the depth slightly for each pass. When ends and sides are to be rabbeted, the ends are done first to prevent splintering of the sides.

Fig. 2-35 Result of rabbeting end grain after sides have been shaped.

Fig. 2-36 Burn marks resulting from too slow a feed when routing.

When using cutters with a pilot, there is a possibility that the pilot will mar the edge of the work. The marring may occur if the feed is too slow or if the router is pressed against the work with too much force. This problem is eliminated completely when the router guide is used. The guide is adjustable and slides against the edge of the work. It may be used on circular work, but not on irregular edges.

Beading and other decorative cuts are made with pilot cutters. If the entire edge is to be shaped, a template or pattern must be attached to the underside of the work piece to guide the pilot.

Fig. 2-37 The adjustable router guide is used for cutting dadoes, rabbets, and grooves.

Fig. 2-38 A beading cutter and cut made with it.

Dadoes and grooves are made by using the router guide or a straightedge clamped firmly to the work. The base of the router is pressed against the straightedge as the cut is made. The guide is positioned so the cutter will be at the desired location. If a blind dado is required, a stop block is placed on the work piece to limit the travel of the router.

Laminated plastics are generally installed with a slight overhang which must be trimmed flush. The router is ideally suited for this task. Special cutters with ball-bearing pilots are made for this purpose. Two cutters are generally used: a flush trimmer and a twenty-two degree trimmer, used to break the sharp edge of the laminate.

Sander

There are two basic types of sanders used in the home shop: the belt and the finishing sander. The belt sander is used primarily for removing stock. It utilizes a continuous belt abrasive, cuts fast, and requires some degree of skill to use. The biggest problem with the belt sander is oversanding. The tool must be kept moving over the work surface continuously. If allowed to rest in one spot

Fig. 2-39 A belt sander in use.

momentarily, it will gouge the work. The machine must be switched on before the belt contacts the work and lifted off the work before stopping the motor. The sander is held evenly over the work and lowered gently. Without applying downward pressure, the sander should be moving forward and backward continuously. After each stroke, the sander should be shifted to the side about half the width of the belt. Before sanding with a finer grit abrasive, the work should be dusted thoroughly.

Finishing sanders are finishing tools. While they will remove some stock, they are mostly used for the final sanding operation after hand or power

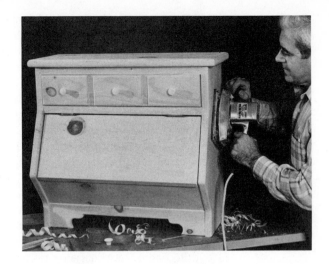

Fig. 2-40 The finishing sander in use.

sanding has taken place. Two types of finishing sanders are made: orbital and oscillating. Of the two, the oscillating will produce the finest finish. In the orbital sander, the platen (and abrasive) moves in a circular motion, making small circles about one-fourth of an inch in diameter and removing some stock. The oscillating sander moves in a straight line, forward and backward, and produces an exceptionally smooth surface. In addition to sanding, the oscillating sander is also used for rubbing down finishes with rubbing compound. Some sanders are made to operate as either type, orbital or oscillating, simply by switching a control lever. The oscillating sander must be moved only in the direction of the wood grain.

Fig. 2-41 Dual-action sander. The lever position determines the mode in use.

ABRASIVES

Most coated abrasives are called *sandpaper.* However, there are various types which, though not containing sand or not containing paper, are nevertheless commonly called *sandpaper.* The term is used here accordingly.

29

The grit on the backing (which may be either paper or cloth) is called the coating. When the grit covers the entire backing surface it is known as closed-coat paper. This paper will clog quickly when used on softwoods. Its chief advantage is that it cuts fast because of the high concentration of abrasive grits. Open-coat papers are those in which only 50 to 70 percent of the surface is coated, leaving some space between each grit to minimize clogging. Open-coat paper is recommended for softwoods and for removing paint. Both open- and closed-coat abrasives are made in various grades, from coarse to very fine.

The abrasives used in woodworking are garnet, flint, aluminum oxide, and silicon carbide. Garnet and flint are natural substances; the others are man-made. Flint is the least desirable, as it is not as tough as the others. Garnet is slightly harder and cuts better. Aluminum oxide and silicon carbide are extremely hard and ideally suited for woodworking. Aluminum oxide should be used for hardwoods, and silicon carbide for softwoods.

Abrasives are graded according to their grit size. Number 4 is very coarse; 10/0, the finest. Very coarse (grit 4 to 2-1/2) should be used for stock removal. This should be followed by coarse (grit 2, 1-1/2, or 1) to remove all marks left by the very coarse grades; then medium (grits 1/2, 1/0, and 2/0), to remove the rough surfaces left by the previous sanding; then fine (grits 3/0, 4/0, and 5/0), for final sanding and before applying the finish coats. Grades 6/0 to 10/0 are used during and after such finishing operations as staining, lacquering, etc. The finest grade, 10/0, is for polishing after all of the finishing materials have been applied.

Hand sanding is not obsolete, as there are times when machine sanding is not practical. For flat surfaces, a block with the paper wrapped tightly around it should always be used. Commercially made blocks are available. Most have some method of gripping the paper. For contour sanding, it may be necessary to make a block to mate with the work piece.

Fig. 2–42 Hand sanding is still useful where machines cannot reach.

Fig. 2-43 Contour sanding with shaped block.

Sanding should only be done with the grain of the wood. Care should be used at the ends and edges, as the tendency is to round off the corners. Paper wrapped around dowels may be used for sanding curved edges. With a drill press, lathe, or other tool with a chuck, sanding discs or drums may be used for sanding curved surfaces. For sanding small diameters, sandpaper may be glued to dowels, which are then chucked.

Flap-type brush-backed sanding sheets are made to be used with portable drills or on an arbor shaft. Useful for irregular surfaces, the brushes will force the abrasive strips into the work piece, no matter what the contour.

Fig. 2-44 Flap-backed sander will sand irregular surfaces smooth.

Since sanding operations in the home workshop are usually limited to small jobs, dust is seldom a problem, except for the nuisance it causes by settling throughout the house. However, fine dust, as produced by sanding, may be a health hazard. Sufficient concentrations of dust, dry weather, and sparks or open flame may cause a violent explosion. This happens all too often in grain elevators, where grain dust explodes with terrifying force. Adequate ventilation, therefore, should be used when sanding, and, if practical, sanding should be done outdoors.

Another problem caused by the fine sanding dust shows up on oil burners. The ignition points will build up an accumulation of dust which may lead to blow backs and other problems. If at all possible, the oil burner area should be closed off to keep it dust-free; but, of course, access should be left for repairs and maintenance work.

STATIONARY POWER TOOLS

Table saws and radial arm saws and sanders are widely used in the modern home shop. Other tools include the bandsaw, jointer, jigsaw, and drill press.

Table Saw

The table saw is also called a bench saw and circular saw. In addition to its main function, which is ripping and crosscutting, the table saw may be used for cutting moldings, rabbeting, dadoing, beveling, cove cutting, mitering, panel raising, and many other chores. Except for some small saws which have tilting tables, most table saws have tilting arbors which permit the blade to be tilted from zero to forty-five degrees.

Fig. 2-45 A typical table saw.

Various blades are available for the saw, each with a specific function. Some have carbide tips and will remain sharper much longer than conventional blades.

Rip cuts (lengthwise cuts through a board) are made with the aid of a fence. The edge of the board contacting the fence must be straight and true. If a board to be ripped has an uneven edge, it must be straightened by some means, such as planing or jointing. If this is not practical, a straightedge, board, or other straight piece may be fastened temporarily to the uneven board to guide it along the fence. A straightedge taped securely to the top edge of the board will not mar the work. If masking tape is used, it must be at least one inch wide and should be taped to the top and bottom edges of the straightedge to prevent movement. Otherwise, nails should be used to hold the pieces.

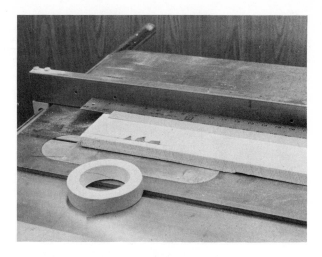

Fig. 2-46 Ripping an irregular edged
board with the aid of a straightedge.

Large pieces are treated differently. Here a straightedge is clamped to the
bottom of the panel and made to ride along the edge of the saw table.

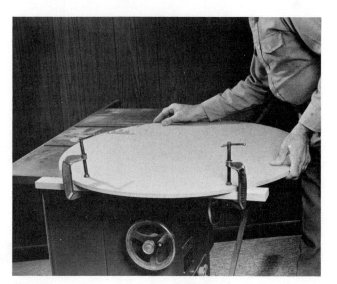

Fig. 2-47 The edge of a table saw
serves as a guide for trimming stock
which cannot be fed along a fence.

For the sake of clarity, it should be noted that most photos show the
table saw in use without the splitter or guard, but these should always be used
except when they will interfere with the job being done. Also, for clarity, the
saw blade is usually photographed with the blade projecting more than the
recommended one-fourth of an inch.

Long pieces being ripped require an outfeed support, which may be
another machine or anything of suitable height. A saw horse may be made for
this purpose, making it one inch lower than the machine height and beveling
the edge slightly so the work will ride onto it.

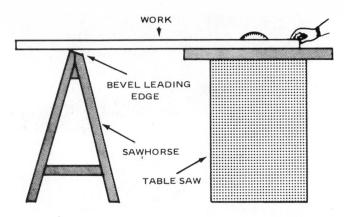

WORK

BEVEL LEADING
EDGE

SAWHORSE

TABLE SAW

Fig. 2-48 Outfeed support for table saw.

When ripping work narrower than three inches, a push stick should be used to keep the fingers safely away from the saw blade. Also, the blade should project one-fourth of an inch above the work surface.

Fig. 2-49 The push stick keeps fingers at a safe distance from the saw blade.

Crosscutting on the table saw is done with the aid of the miter gauge. The work is held snugly against the gauge, and both are advanced toward the blade. A mark scribed on the table insert to indicate the edge of the blade is useful for positioning the work in crosscutting.

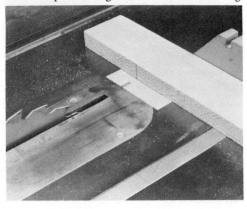

Fig. 2-50 Kerf marks on the saw table permit alignment of the stock to be cut.

Stops are used when duplicate pieces must be cut. They may be clamped to the fence, to the table, or to an auxiliary wood facing fastened to the miter gauge. It should be noted that the stops, if clamped to the table or fence, are placed well forward of the blade. To prevent the free end from binding, it is important that the work be free of the stop as it enters the blade.

*Fig. 2-51 A safe method of cutting
duplicate pieces on the table saw.*

When crosscutting small pieces, it may be necessary to clamp the piece piggyback to a larger one which is held against the miter gauge. When crosscutting wide boards, it may be necessary to reverse the miter gauge so that it will be ahead of the leading edge of the board.

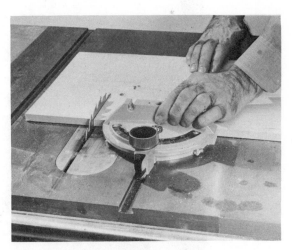

*Fig. 2-52 When boards are too wide, the
miter gauge may be used in reverse.*

Miters are cut with the miter gauge in a manner similar to crosscutting. However, the work has a tendency to creep when making such cuts. To minimize this tendency, the work should be held tightly as it is fed. On hardwoods, this may not be enough, for no matter how tightly the piece is held, it will creep

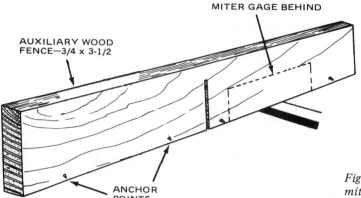

AUXILIARY WOOD
FENCE—3/4 x 3-1/2

MITER GAGE BEHIND

ANCHOR
POINTS

Fig. 2-53 Points on the
miter gauge board prevent
creep when mitering.

and spoil the job. One positive method of overcoming this problem is to use
anchor points on the wood facing of the miter gauge. The points, which may be
made to disappear when not needed, pierce the work and prevent lateral movement of the work piece. If the pinpricks made in the edge of the work are objectionable, masking tape may be fastened to the work and miter gauge or wood
facing. When mitering crown moldings, a stop may be used to hold the work at
the proper angle. The stop should be clamped to the miter gauge facing.

Fig. 2-54 Taping work to a
miter gauge is an alternate
method of preventing creep.

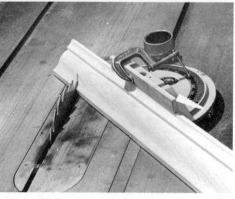

Fig. 2-55 Blocking molding for
a compound miter is accomplished with a strip of wood and
a small clamp.

Rabbeting on the table saw is performed in two operations. First, the saw blade depth and fence should be set to produce the desired cut. The piece should then be stood on edge and the first cut made. Next, the fence and blade depth should be reset and the second cut made with the work flat on the table. The user should stand to one side of the blade, as the trapped waste could shoot back with considerable force.

Fig. 2-56 First cut. Work is held vertically for the first cut when rabbeting on the table saw.

Fig. 2-57 The second cut is made with the work held horizontally.

Grooving and dadoing on the table saw may be done by making a series of passes through the blade until the desired width is obtained. A better and more efficient method is to use the dado head. This is simply a thick saw blade which may be adjusted to various widths. Some dado heads consist of a series of blades which are sandwiched on the saw arbor. Spacers are used to obtain the desired width. An adjustable dado head which may be "dialed" to obtain the desired cutting width is also available.

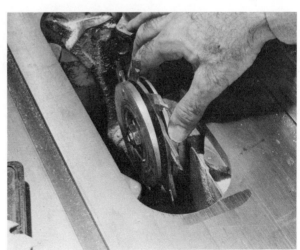

Fig. 2-58 "Dialing" a dado. The adjustable blade permits cuts from 1/4 to 13/16 of an inch wide.

In use, the dado head is treated like a regular blade, but because of the extra width of the cuts, special table inserts are required. If the slot in your table insert is not wide enough for a dado blade, simply trace the insert's outline onto a piece of plywood and make a cutout wide enough to clear the dado blade. Use this plywood substitute instead of the insert furnished with the machine. The work may be fed along the fence or with the miter gauge. Since more stock is removed with the dado blade, the work should be fed at a slow rate.

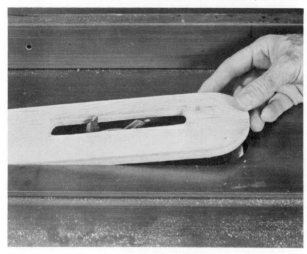

Fig. 2-59 A wide-slotted table insert must be used with dado blades. This one is made of plywood.

Rabbeting with a dado blade requires the use of a wood facing fastened to the regular fence. The procedure is as follows. The dado blade is lowered below the table surface, and a board is then fastened to the fence, positioned as required. The machine is turned on, and with the blade turning, it is raised so it cuts into the board, avoiding cutting the metal fence. The blade is then raised to the height required for the rabbet, and the work is fed in the normal manner.

Fig. 2-60 An auxiliary wood fence is necessary when using the dado blade for rabbeting.

Raised panels are often used on cabinet doors. The table saw is ideally suited for panel raising, either with a molding head or with a regular blade. When the molding head is used, the work is held flat on the table and the saw arbor is tilted sufficiently to produce the desired bevel. A straight cutter is used in the molding head. When raising panels with a regular saw blade, the work is held on edge, and the blade is tilted slightly and raised to the desired height. The fence is set as needed, and then the work is fed slowly while it is held firmly against the fence.

Fig. 2-61 Making a raised panel insert on the table saw.

Long-lasting carbide-tipped blades are available for both the table and radial arm saws.

Fig. 2-62 A carbide-tipped blade for use on a table or radial arm saw.

Radial Arm Saw

The radial arm saw is quite a machine. Some of its uses include crosscutting, ripping, mitering, beveling, dadoing, rabbeting, sanding, and shaping. For normal crosscutting operations, the fence should be in the forward position.

Fig. 2-63 Crosscutting on the radial arm saw. The semicircular cuts at the edge of the auxiliary table prevent sawdust buildup along the backstop.

For wide boards or for gang cutting, the fence is moved to the rear position. Some saws may be fitted with arm extensions, which increase the capacity of the machine.

Fig. 2-64 Extension increases the capacity of the radial arm.

If duplicate pieces are to be cut, a stop block clamped to the fence is used.

Fig. 2-65 A stop is clamped to the backstop when cutting duplicate pieces.

Splintering on the underside of the work piece usually occurs when the blade clearance groove in the table top wears and becomes too wide. To minimize the splintering, the table top is covered with a piece of quarter-inch plywood. A scrap piece of wall paneling is suitable. When the plywood begins to wear, it may be replaced. The plywood should be attached with brads that are not in line with the saw blade. The heads are then sunk slightly. To eliminate the nails completely, double-faced tape may be used.

Fig. 2-66 A plywood top fastened to the saw table will ensure splinter-free cuts. Replace when the kerf groove wears too wide.

Mitering on the radial arm saw will cause the work to creep just as it does on the table saw. Fence anchor points, pointed screws driven from the rear of the fence, will prevent creep. The points should protrude slightly from the front

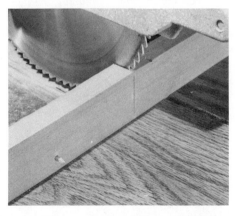

Fig. 2-67 Pointed screws serve as anchor points. They may be backed off when not being used for mitering.

where they will prevent lateral movement of the work piece. When not mitering, the screws should be backed off slightly. Instead of the anchor points, masking

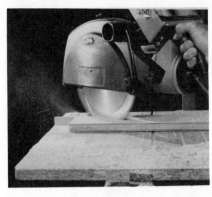

Fig. 2-68 Mitered work will not creep if anchor points are used.

tape may be used, as suggested for the table saw. The tape is run along the fence, with half of its width on the fence and the other half on the work.

Ripping on the radial arm saw requires that the blade travel parallel to the fence. In the crosscutting operation, the thrust from the blade forces the work down and against the fence. In ripping, care must be taken that the work is fed into the rotation of the blade. Except for ripping wide boards, the in-rip position is normally used. In this position, the yoke is rotated 90 degrees, with the motor placed on the outside with the blade inside toward the fence. The carriage is locked in position, and the blade guard is adjusted and lowered as much as possible on the infeed side. The antikickback device must also be set at this time. The work is fed with one edge riding against the fence. Fingers should be kept well away from the blade and a push stick used on narrow stock.

Beveling on the radial arm saw falls into two categories: bevel-crosscutting and bevel-ripping. The procedure for these cuts is the same as in straight work. The blade must be tilted in a downward position to the desired bevel, then locked. For compound cuts, the arm is swung to the desired angle in addition to tilting the blade.

Taper ripping is often used in the construction of furniture legs. A simple jig is required for this technique. The jig may also be used for cutting tapers on the table saw. The jig is made to suit the work at hand. For different tapers, the jig will have to be made accordingly. After dressing the stock to size, one end of the work is placed into the first notch of the jig, and then both the jig and the work are fed through the blade. If the work is to be tapered on all sides, an adjacent side is cut in a similar manner. Then, with the work in the second notch of the jig, the remaining two sides are cut.

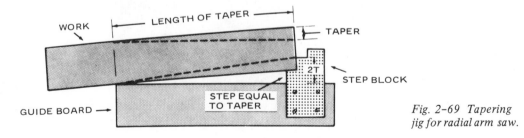

Fig. 2-69 Tapering jig for radial arm saw.

The dado head for the table saw may also be used on the radial arm saw. Paper spacers are placed between the blades to control the width of the cut. Plain dadoes are cut in the same manner as crosscutting: the blade is lowered to produce the desired depth of cut. For blind dadoes, as used when installing shelving, a stop clamped to the saw arm is used to limit the length of the cut.

Fig. 2-70 Blind dadoes or other cuts are controlled by clamping a stop block to the arm of the saw.

End laps and cross laps are easily made with the dado head. Both pieces of stock are cut simultaneously. The depth of the cut must be one-half of the thickness of the stock. The width of the dado is the same as the stock width. This may require several passes of the dado cutter.

A mitering jig, consisting of two cleats mounted to a piece of plywood, will greatly simplify the making of consistently accurate miters. The cleats

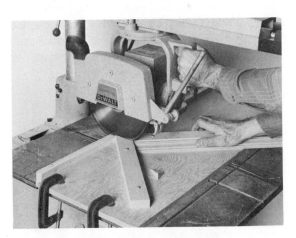

Fig. 2-71 An easily made mitering jig.

are fastened with screws to permit fine adjustments. Once adjusted, a few nails are driven into each cleat. In use, the jig is clamped to the saw table. The same jig may be used on the table saw by adding a pair of hardwood slides to ride in the table grooves.

Drill Press

Of all the stationary tools, the drill press is one of the easiest to use. Its primary function is to bore holes, but it may be put to other uses as well. Most drill presses have cone pulleys which make it possible to select various spindle speeds. Depending on the motor used, speeds vary from about 300 RPM to more than 5,000 RPM. The outstanding feature of these machines is their accuracy. Holes are bored perfectly straight and square, and the depth is controlled precisely.

Fig. 2-72 The drill is unsurpassed for boring straight, accurate holes.

It should be noted that normally holes are *bored* in wood and *drilled* in steel, but the terms are used interchangeably, and either is correct. Also, the cutting tool used for wood is called a *bit,* and the tool for steel is called a *drill.* A wood bit cannot be used on steel, but a drill can be used on wood. In addition to boring holes in wood and steel, the drill press may also be used for cutting plugs, mortising, sanding, grinding, and routing.

Fig. 2-73 Proper tool speed is determined by the size of holes and the type of stock being bored.

The speed at which bits are used depends on such factors as bit size, wood density, and grain. Therefore, it is impossible to state specific cutting speeds. Normally, spur bits up to three-fourths of an inch in diameter are used at speeds between 2,000 and 3,000 RPM. The larger the bit, the slower the speed. Using a wood pad on the drill press table makes it possible to produce clean-cut holes without splintering on the underside. The depth stop on the drill permits boring holes to an exact depth. This is especially useful when countersinking or counterboring holes for screws, buttons, and plugs.

Fig. 2-74 Most drill presses have depth-control stops.

Often in the home workshop a certain size screw may not be available. In such cases, the screw at hand may be used. An appropriate hole is counterbored so the screw will penetrate the second piece as required.

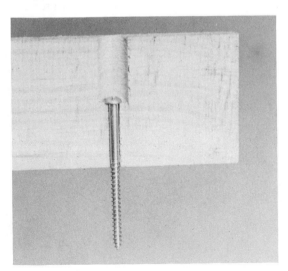

Fig. 2-75 A method of installing screws in thick stock.

Angular drilling is accomplished by tilting the drill table or, in the case of fixed tables, tilting the "line of work." For small pieces, a tilting vise may be

Fig. 2-76 A tilting table permits angular drilling.

used. Work may be tilted in various ways. Wedges and props are useful. A simple adjustable tilting table accessory may be made. For drilling pocket holes in rails (used for fastening table tops), an angular jig is useful. The jig should be cut to hold the work securely and at the proper angle; then, if necessary, it is clamped to the table. A spur bit is used first to make the pocket hole. Then a smaller bit is used for the screw clearance.

Fig. 2-77 A jig made for drilling pocket holes in a rail.

To drill holes in round stock, a V-block cut from an appropriate piece of lumber is employed. Two forty-five-degree cuts are made in the block, which is then located and clamped so that the bit is centered over the center of the V-cut. Round stock to be drilled will be automatically centered.

Fig. 2-78 V-block for drilling into the edge of round stock. The backstop supports the piece.

When a series of holes are to be made in a straight line, a fence clamped to the table is used. The fence may also be used to bore a mortise using a spur bit. Overlapping holes are then bored with the bit set to the proper depth, the quill is locked, and the work is pushed through the drill to clean out the mortise.

Fig. 2-79 The first step in mortising on the drill press consists of making a series of overlapping holes.

Fig. 2-80 After holes have been bored, the quill is locked in position, and work is slowly fed through a cutter to clean out the mortise.

To bore holes accurately into dowels, a jig may be used. The dowel size hole is bored into a wood block. A saw cut and set screw will permit tightening the jig around the dowel as shown in Figure 2-81.

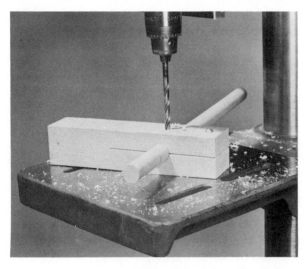

Fig. 2-81 A jig for boring holes in dowels.

Contour sanding on the drill press is done with the aid of a drum sander and an auxiliary table, which is simply a flat board bolted to the table. A clearance hole in the center permits the sanding drum to be lowered below the surface. In use, the quill of the machine is lowered with the drum a trifle below the surface and locked in position. The work is fed against the drum while moving it from left to right. Although straight pieces may be sanded this way, this method is generally used to sand contoured stock.

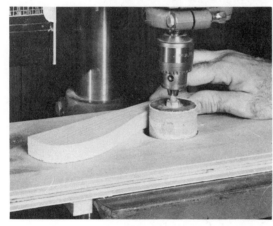

Fig. 2-82 Using the drill press for contour sanding.

Some routing operations may be performed on the drill press. A special router bit adapter is used for this purpose. A regular Jacobs chuck may be used to hold the bit for occasional work. The bit must have a half-inch shank, and the machine should be run at high speeds. The work is always fed against a fence.

With the fence behind the cutter, the work must be fed from left to right. Shallow cuts one-eighth of an inch or less should be made in each pass. For deeper cuts, the passes are repeated, deepening the cut each time. Round work may be grooved by using a curved fence.

Plug cutting on the drill press is done with the aid of plug cutters, which are available in numerous sizes. Plugs are commonly used to conceal screws in furniture and other woodwork. They are normally cut from the same species of wood as the piece to be plugged; however, contrasting wood may be used if desired. The cutter may be fed completely through the work. The cut plugs will

Fig. 2-83 Cutting plugs requires a sharp tool.

feed up and eject from the tool. Most workers prefer to cut partially into the stock. The pieces are then sliced off on the table saw.

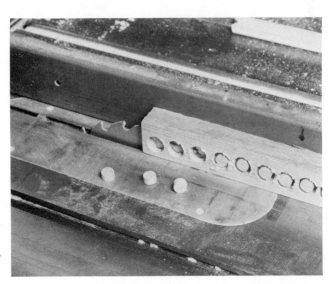

Fig. 2-84 Sawing frees the plugs from the stock.

Stationary Sanders

Stationary sanders are of two types: belt and disc, or a combination of both. Of the belt type, two versions are commonly used in the home shop: the wide-belt and the narrow-belt. The wide-belt sander is generally used for sanding flat stock. However, the curved part of the belt around the drum may also be used for contoured pieces. The narrow-belt sander, better known as a sander/grinder, has a one-inch-wide belt which has many uses in the shop.

Fig. 2-85 The belt sander has adjustable work support.

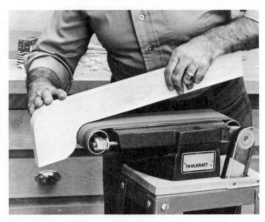

Fig. 2-86 Using the end drum to sand curved stock.

Although small in size, it is capable of handling many large and small sanding jobs. With various jigs the narrow-belt sander may be used for beveling, rounding, and even pattern sanding.

Fig. 2-87 The sander/grinder uses belts one inch wide which may be stripped to narrower widths if necessary.

Fig. 2-88 A jig for sanding bevels at ends
of stock is clamped to the sander table.

To edge sand round discs, a plywood platen is clamped to the sander table. A pivot point (cut from a nail) is then inserted a distance from the abrasive equal to the radius of the circle. Only one clamp should be tightened partially at this

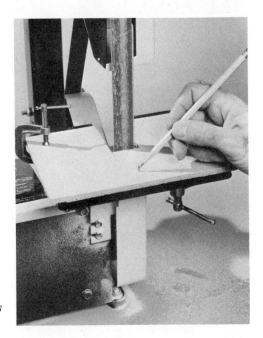

Fig 2-89 The nail point projecting from the table pad serves
as a pivot for sanding discs.

time. The rough-cut disc is fastened onto the pivot point, and, with the power on, the work and auxiliary table are swung into place. Then the second clamp is tightened and the work is rotated slowly on the pivot point. The result is a perfectly round and smooth disc.

51

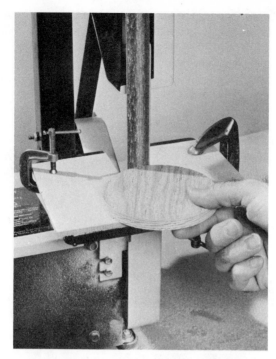

Fig. 2-90 Work is rotated on the pivot to produce a perfectly round circle.

The stationary sander may also be used to do a sort of turning on small stock. The work piece is chucked into a portable drill. The sander and drill are then turned on, and the work is shaped by manipulating the drill. Since both tools are rotating, the cutting action is fast, and the results are fairly good.

Fig. 2-91 The sander and drill are used to shape the end of the stock.

Power Miter Saw

    The power miter saw is gaining popularity among the home workshoppers. Primarily a cutoff saw for contractors, the tool is easy to use, and the cuts produced with it are surprisingly accurate. To miter crown moldings, a support

Fig. 2-92 A power miter saw may be set to miters from zero to forty-five degrees.

Fig. 2-93 Some of the cuts made with the miter saw.

strip beveled to match the molding in its mounting angle is fastened to the saw backstop. The support may be held with screws driven through the backstop or with double-faced tape.

Fig. 2-94 Support is fastened to the backstop of the saw when cutting crown molding.

Although not covered here, other stationary tools are used in furniture making. These include the bandsaw, jigsaw, shaper, and jointer. Any serious woodworker will do well to familiarize himself with these tools, as well as those already discussed in this chapter.

Chapter 3

CONSTRUCTION TECHNIQUES

Building furniture requires some degree of layout work. In its simplest form, this may consist of marking a line on the edge of a board. Some jobs, of course, are more complex and require the layout of curves, angles, templates, and other geometric shapes. Regardless of the layout operation involved, it should be done accurately if a good piece of work is to be the result.

When measuring stock, the end of the board must be straight and square. Often board ends are rough cut at the lumber yard or mill with little care taken to ensure that the stock is square. Whether a board is being sawed by hand or by machine, a line should be squared across the face of the board. The line is necessary for hand sawing, but it will serve as a check on the adjustment of the machine in the case of a table saw or radial arm saw. Thin lines make for greater accuracy. To gauge a line parallel to an edge, a marking gauge is used. A combination square may also be used for this purpose. The head is locked at the desired location, then a pencil is run along the end of the rule as the tool is slid along the work.

There are various methods of drawing arcs and circles. The compass and divider are generally used for circles of up to twelve inches in diameter. For larger sizes, a pair of trammel points must be used. If the mark left by the center leg of the divider or trammel point is objectionable, a thin piece of wood or plastic may be taped over the area to prevent marring the work. For some jobs requiring rounded corners, a round object, such as a can or jar, may be traced.

Often it is advisable to make a layout on paper, especially for intricate work. This eliminates construction lines, pin holes, and other marks on the work. Kraft paper is excellent for this purpose. If the layout is not too large, file folder stock is even better, as the lines show up clearer than on kraft and the stock is easily cut with a scissors or knife. After cutting, the pattern is traced onto the work.

Fig. 3-1 A can substitutes for a compass when drawing arcs.

Ellipses or oval layouts may be accomplished by several methods. The simplest involves the use of three pins and a string. The ellipse consists of two axes of different lengths at right angles to each other. The major and minor axes are drawn and marked A-B and C-D. A divider is set to measure one-half of the major diameter. One leg of the divider is placed at point C, and arcs X and Y are struck. Pins are placed at points X, Y, and C. A string is tied tautly around the three pins, and then pin C is removed. A pencil is held vertically at the point where pin C was located, and, while keeping the string taut, the pencil is moved around the board, resulting in a perfect oval.

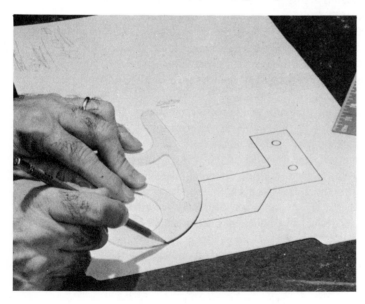

Fig. 3-2 Layout being made on file folder stock.

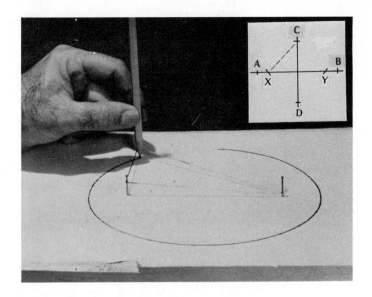

Fig. 3-3 A simple method of drawing an ellipse.

To create a hexagon, a circle is first drawn. Then, with the same setting on the divider, the circumference of the circle is stepped off six times. The points of intersection are connected to form the hexagon. For an equilateral triangle, every other point is connected.

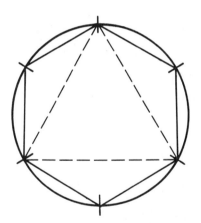

Fig. 3-4 The hexagon is drawn with the aid of a divider.

Another way to draw a triangle is to draw a base line AB. Then, using the base line as a radius, scribe intersecting arcs AC and BC. The points A, B, and C are connected to form an equilateral triangle.

Angles are laid out with a protractor. The base line of the protractor is placed on a pencil line which has a mark drawn to indicate its center. The center of the protractor is aligned over the mark, and then the desired angle is picked out along the circumference of the instrument. The two marks are connected to form the angle. If the angle is to be transferred to a tool or to be marked on a piece of stock, the T-bevel is used.

Enlarging drawings to full size is usually done by the use of square grids. This method is excellent for transferring or enlarging irregular outlines. The drawing to be reproduced will have grid lines crossing it vertically and horizontally. A notation on the drawing will indicate the size of the squares to be drawn. For example, the notation may read "all squares three-fourths of an inch." This means the number of lines shown must be duplicated and drawn three-fourths of an inch apart. To make the layout, a pencil mark is placed on each grid line at those points where a line crosses that same grid line in the original layout. After all the points have been marked, they are connected by drawing a pencil through each point. The lines are then trued up, using a French curve if necessary. Now the layout may be cut and traced onto the work, or transferred with carbon paper.

WOOD JOINTS

Numerous joints, simple and complex, are used to fasten wood parts in furniture making. Many joints are held with glue alone, but some require the addition of dowels, splines, screws, and other fasteners to increase their strength. Regardless of the type of joint used, it is essential that the parts fit together well; otherwise a weak joint will result.

Butt Joints

Commonly used for fastening wood members, butt joints are the easiest to make and also the weakest of joints. By butting one piece up against another, a butt joint is made. This joint may be greatly improved by the use of dowels. Other methods of reinforcing the butt joint include glue blocks, corner blocks, and gussets. Metal corner blocks are often used to reinforce chair and table legs.

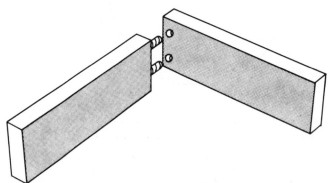

Fig. 3–5 The plain butt joint is usually reinforced with dowels.

Rabbet Joints.

Strong and easy to make, rabbet joints are widely used for drawer construction. They may be cut in one or both pieces to be joined. To minimize end

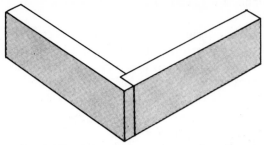

Fig. 3-6 The rabbet joint is
widely used in woodworking.

grain, a deep rabbet may be utilized. This joint is somewhat weaker than the
conventional rabbet which has a width equal to the stock thickness and a depth
of one-half of the thickness.

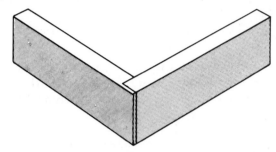

Fig. 3-7 The deep rabbet
effectively minimizes end
grain.

Rabbet joints are also useful for installing the back panels of cabinets.
When the back is to be installed into a chest, bookcase, or similar piece, the
depth of the rabbet is cut to the same thickness as the back panel. For base
and wall cabinets, such as kitchen cabinets or built-ins, the rabbet is cut deeper
to allow for trimming the side panels to fit any discrepancies in the wall.

Fig. 3-8 Typical method of
installing cabinet backs.

Rabbet edge joints consist of two similar rabbets cut from opposite surfaces along the length of a board.

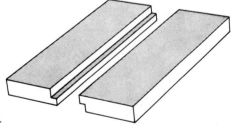

Fig. 3-9 A rabbet-edge joint.

Dado and Groove Joints

The dado is a square groove cut across the grain of the wood. When cut with the grain along the length of a board, it is known as a groove or plough cut. A blind dado is used when the appearance of the plain dado would be objectionable, such as on the front edge of a cabinet. It should stop about one-half of an inch from the front edge of its mating part.

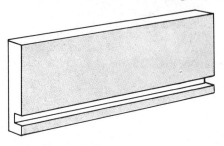

Fig. 3-10 A dado runs across the width of a board, and a groove runs lengthwise.

When added strength and rigidity are needed, a rabbet and dado are combined. Here the rabbet acts like a tenon. This joint may also be made with a half dovetail or full dovetail, which is a very strong locking joint.

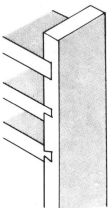

Fig 3-11 Three popular joints: top—dado; center—rabbeted dado; and bottom—dovetail.

Corner dadoes are often used to support shelves on tables or for stretchers, as found on butler tray tables. The groove is cut across the corner, forming a triangular cross section.

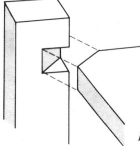

Fig. 3-12 The corner dado.

When laying out boards for dado joints, the opposite sides are clamped together and the pieces laid out as a unit. This ensures alignment of the parts when assembling.

Fig. 3-13 A good way to lay out dadoes.

Spline Edge Joints

Often used when strength is a requirement, the spline edge joint consists of a groove cut along the edge of two pieces to be joined. The groove is usually one-eighth or one-fourth of an inch wide. A spline having the same width as the groove is cut from a piece of plywood and inserted into both grooves. If solid wood is used for the spline, its grain should run crosswise to the length of the groove.

Cutting the spline groove on edge may be done on the table saw, radial arm saw, or router. The groove is usually placed closer to the inside corner of the miter. Of the various methods used to cut the groove, the table saw is the easiest. The blade is tilted forty-five degrees, and the work is fed using both the miter gauge and the fence.

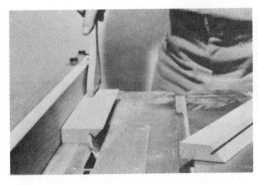

Fig. 3-14 Cutting a spline on the table saw.

Dowels

Used to strengthen various joints, dowels also aid in the alignment of mating pieces when clamping, although this is not their primary function. Doweled joints are commonly used by home craftsmen because they are easy to make and assemble. Butt, edge, and miter joints may all be strengthened with dowels.

Fig. 3-15 A doweled miter joint.

The dowels used for joints are available as pins in various diameters and lengths. They are grooved and usually made of maple or birch. The grooves serve two purposes: they allow air to escape from the bottom of the hole into which the dowel is driven, and they provide better holding power. It is important that dowels be kept in a dry area until used. A dowel with a high moisture content when installed will eventually dry out and shrink, causing joint failure. The ends of the dowel should be beveled to prevent mushrooming by the hammerhead when being driven into the dowel hole.

Fig. 3-16 Spiral grooved dowels permit air to escape as they are driven into a hole.

There are many ways to locate dowels. One popular method utilizes dowel centers; another, the doweling jig. Dowel centers have a pointed end which permits the transfer of the hole location in one piece to another. The procedure in using the centers follows. The dowel holes are located and bored in the first piece, with the holes at right angles to the wood surface. The dowel centers are inserted and then the mating pieces are brought together carefully to transfer the hole positions to the second piece. The holes are bored one-eighth of an inch deeper than one-half of the dowel length.

Fig. 3-17 A properly installed dowel must not touch the bottom of a hole.

The self-centering dowel jig is a time saver, but more important, its use ensures squarely bored holes—perfectly aligned and centered. In using the doweling jig, the boards to be doweled are held together on edge. A pencil line is gauged across the pieces at each dowel location. The dowel jig is then aligned by matching its index mark with the pencil line on the piece to be bored. Tightening the tool will automatically center it. A drill is then inserted into the hardened bushing, and the hole is bored to the desired depth. The process is repeated for the remaining holes in each board.

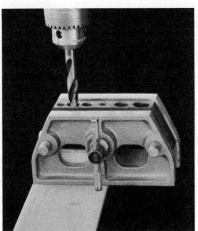

Fig. 3-18 A self-centering dowel jig.

Dowels may be used to reinforce end grain when making screwed joints. The dowel should be located so that the threads of the screw pass completely through it.

Miter Joints

Commonly used in furniture making, miter joints are used to conceal the end grain of both pieces to be joined. Used by themselves, such joints are rather weak; therefore, they are usually reinforced by such means as dowels, keys, splines, screws, or nails.

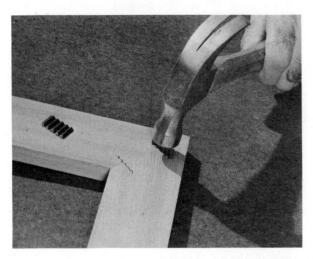

Fig. 3-19 Reinforcing flat miter with wavy nails.

Flat miters are often reinforced with keys (also called feathers) which are fitted into the outer edge of the joint.

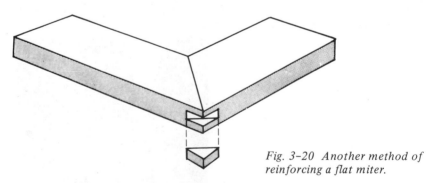

Fig. 3-20 Another method of reinforcing a flat miter.

In addition to strengthening the joint, the use of any of these devices helps maintain alignment of the parts when gluing. Splines may be made of wood, plywood, hardboard, or metal. As a rule, wood splines should be used for solid lumber miters, and plywood or hardboard for plywood miters. Metal splines may be used for either material. Solid wood splines must be cross-grained;

otherwise, they have a good chance of splitting. Grooves for the spline must be carefully cut; the table saw is usually used for this purpose.

When grooving the flat miter on the table saw, the·blade is set to the proper height, and then the fence is adjusted so the groove will be centered. The opening in the table insert should be small enough to prevent the work from falling through. The work is fed in an upright position while sliding it against the fence. The face side for each piece must face the same direction, either toward or away from the fence. Otherwise, the mating pieces will not lie flush if the saw cut is not exactly centered. A piece of wood clamped to the piece being mitered is made to "ride" the fence on narrow work.

Fig. 3-21 Flat miter rides fence when being splined.

Clamp nails are patented devices which fit into a twenty-two-gauge kerf cut into the mitered edge. The flanges at the edge of the nail will draw the joint tight as the device is hammered into the work. Clamp nails may also be used on straight and butt joints.

Fig. 3-22 The clamp nail is designed to pull the joint tight.

When grooving a miter to take a key, the work is held with the miter surface perpendicular to the saw table.

The offset miter joint is excellent for cabinet bases and casework. It is very strong because of the large glue surface inherent in its design. The joint is easily made on the table saw, radial arm saw, or shaper.

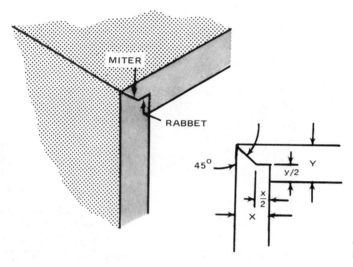

Fig. 3-23 Details of an offset miter joint.

The lap-miter joint combines both the lap joint and the miter joint. It is easily made and used often on cabinet doors.

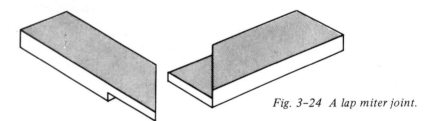

Fig. 3-24 A lap miter joint.

GLUING AND CLAMPING TECHNIQUES

Modern adhesives are available for all types of gluing jobs. Some adhesives are waterproof, while others are highly heat resistant. Some require clamping while setting, and others do not. For best results, the most appropriate glue is selected for the job at hand, and the manufacturer's instructions for application are followed.

Some adhesives contain solvents which may be injurious to one's health if improperly handled. If the instructions recommend using the product with adequate ventilation, they should be followed precisely.

Some adhesives are flammable and must be handled very carefully. For instance, vapors from contact cement are highly explosive. Great care must be

Fig 3-25 Woodworking adhesives.

used with any of these materials. All flames must be extinguished, including pilot lights. No smoking rules should be observed completely, and electrical equipment should not be used while adhesive vapors are present, since the spark from an electric switch may be enough to cause an explosion.

Adhesives

Brief descriptions of the more common adhesives used in woodworking follow.

Contact cement is a liquid of creamy consistency. It is applied with a brush or spreader to both surfaces to be glued. It is air dried for about fifteen minutes, and then both surfaces are brought together precisely, since they will bond instantly on contact. This cement is widely used for bonding laminates to countertops and tabletops.

Liquid resin is a polyvinyl emulsion glue, better known as "white" glue. It comes ready to use in squeeze bottles and in larger economical containers. It is a fast-setting, nonwaterproof glue suitable for wood, leather, cork, and similar materials. It is not recommended for use in areas of high humidity or high temperature.

Plastic resin comes in powdered form and is mixed with water before use. Water-, mold-, and rot-resistant, it is used for wood, particleboard, veneer, etc.— and always with clamps. For best results, glues that require mixing should be weighed to obtain the proper proportions. A gram scale is ideal for this purpose.

Fig. 3-26 Proper proportions of glue powder and water are ensured when weighed.

Powdered casein is a strong, water-resistant glue ideally suited for use on oily woods, such as teak. It is mixed with water and sets at low temperatures.

Resorcinol is a waterproof glue used when structural strength is required. It is generally supplied in two parts which must be combined before use. It has a dark red color and requires clamping while setting.

Liquid glues are made from the heads, skins, and bones of fish. Though they provide a good strong joint suitable for furniture making, they are not recommended for use in areas of high dampness.

Aliphatic resin glue is similar in appearance to white glue, except that it has an off-white color. It has some advantages over white glue, however. Alphatic resin glue has more tack, dries fast, and makes a much stronger joint. Also, the parts being glued have less tendency to slide when clamping pressure is applied. Like white glue, it has poor moisture resistance and is to be used for interior work only.

Gluing Joints

There are certain basic rules which should be followed when making glued joints. Clamps and clamp pads should be on hand, adjusted, and ready to use. Parts must be checked for good fit; if necessary, the joint should be corrected so all parts will fit tightly. Number or otherwise identify the parts so they may be assembled properly and quickly.

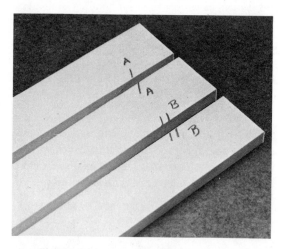

Fig. 3-27 Numbered parts prevent mixups when gluing.

The moisture content of the parts to be joined must be equal and they must be fairly dry. Wood that is glued with too high a moisture content will result in a poor joint. At the other extreme, wood that is very dry will absorb too much moisture from the glue, which also will result in a weak joint.

Most glues form a raised glue line due to swelling caused by moisture from the glue around the joint area. If the work is sanded or machined before the swelling goes down, a depressed joint will result.

Glue should be spread by whatever means is convenient. For some parts, a small, stiff brush or stick will do. For large areas, a paint brush or a roller with a short, stiff nap may be used. White glue should be thinned slightly if large areas are to be glued. The glue should be spread on one or both surfaces and allowed to air dry for a minute or two before the parts are brought together.

Fig. 3-28 Applying glue with a roller.

Since sliding may result in offset joints, care should be taken that this does not happen. If there is waste stock at the ends of the parts, a nail driven angularly at each end will help to prevent sliding.

Fig. 3-29 The nail prevents the sliding of the parts being joined.

Otherwise, strips of wood should be clamped at each end of the assembly. These clamps should not be overtightened, however, as they may prevent the main clamps from functioning properly.

Fig. 3-30 Clamped sticks prevent glued boards from shifting.

Another method that works very well utilizes brad points to prevent sliding. Eighteen-gauge brads are cut diagonally with a pliers, leaving the pointed end about one-fourth of an inch long. The pointed end is held with a pliers and the cut end is forced into the surface to be glued. About 3/32 of an inch of the point is left protruding from the surface. Glue is applied in the normal manner, and the aligned parts are brought together. When clamping pressure is applied, the parts will not shift or slide.

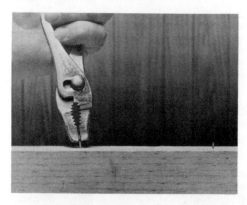

Fig. 3-31 Brad points being inserted along the glue joint.

The grain in edge-glued pieces should run in the same direction. Wide boards should be made up by gluing pieces no wider than six inches, and the growth rings in alternate pieces should run in opposite directions.

Starved joints—which result when too little glue is used or when too much clamping pressure is applied—should be avoided. Excess pressure may force too much glue out of the joint. This is why glue is allowed to air dry and become tacky before parts are joined. The glue will not be so runny and, therefore, will be less likely to be squeezed out of the joint.

Fig. 3-32 Excessive clamp pressure may squeeze out too much glue.

Squeeze-out should not be wiped or removed until after the glue has set. This is especially important if the piece is to be stained. Wiping the glue when it is wet will force it into the pores of the wood, thus acting like a sizing. When stain is applied later on to the piece, the wiped part will not take the stain well. The dried glue pips should be removed with a scraper and then sanded smooth.

Fig. 3-33 A glue spot will not take stain.

Clamping

Clamps should be applied with ample but not excessive pressure. When the glue starts to ooze out of the joint, the pressure is usually sufficient. Cauls are used under the clamp jaws to prevent clamp marks on the work.

Fig. 3-34 Cauls under clamps protect the work surface.

If hand-screw clamps (parallel clamps) are used, the jaws must be parallel to each other, unless the work is angular.

Fig. 3-35 Screw clamps on angular work.

Except for those assembled with clamp nails, all miters must be clamped while the glue sets. There are various ways to do this. Special devices are commercially available but are costly, and unless a lot of miter clamping is anticipated, other means should be used. One method which works very well utilizes miter blocks, which are made from scrap plywood. These blocks are clamped to

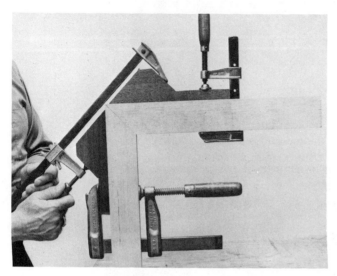

Fig. 3-36 A novel method of clamping miters.

the work piece to form parallel surfaces. Then the blocks are clamped forcing the miter faces tightly together. A band clamp may also be used to draw in the miters. Four corner blocks cut from plywood are placed at the corners of the work with a band clamp tightened around them. For wide-board miters, hardwood pieces beveled forty-five degrees on one edge are lightly glued to the work and serve as bearing surfaces for the miter clamping. After the glue has set, the strips are knocked off and the surface is sanded to remove all traces of the glue.

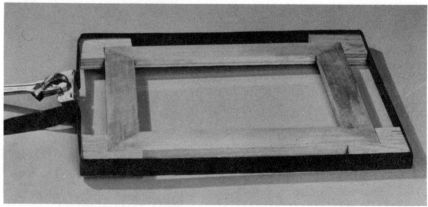

Fig. 3-37 Band clamp and corner blocks aid in clamping the mitered frame.

Fig. 3-38 Clamping a long miter with glue blocks.

An adjustable mitering frame may be made to clamp various sizes of mitered frames. A series of equally spaced holes are drilled into four diagonal strips of hardwood. Corner blocks are made with a clearance at the inside corner, which prevents glue from sticking to them. The clamp bearers are bolted loosely to enable the unit to self-adjust.

Fig. 3-39 An adjustable mitering jig.

When assembling raised panel door frames, glue should not be used to hold the panel. The panel should float freely within the frame to allow it to expand and contract with the weather. The same applies to drawer bottoms.

Assembling Sequence

When gluing mitered frames with dowels or blind splines, the sections must be assembled properly. If three adjacent parts are assembled in sequence, the last piece will be "locked out," and final assembly will be impossible. The proper procedure calls for assembling two opposite corners. The two L-shaped assemblies are then joined.

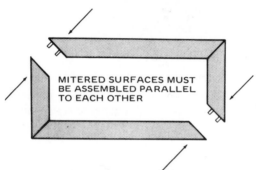

MITERED SURFACES MUST
BE ASSEMBLED PARALLEL
TO EACH OTHER

Fig. 3-40 The proper method of assembling a doweled frame.

This principle also applies when gluing and assembling the framework for cabinets. Stiles and rails should be assembled in a manner that will prevent sections from being locked out. Assembling the parts dry ensures that the materials are in the proper sequence. The pieces may then be numbered in the order of assembly.

When gluing doweled assemblies, glue should not be applied directly to the dowel, as it will be wiped off when the dowel is driven down into the hole. Instead, the glue is applied to the walls of the hole with a small brush before inserting the dowel.

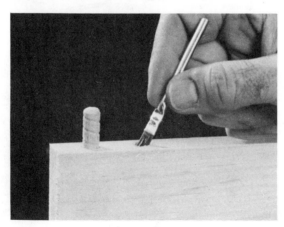

Fig. 3-41 Applying glue to a dowel hole.

Gluing End Grain

End grain poses a problem when gluing. Because of its porosity, end grain absorbs glue readily, thus causing a weak joint. For a stronger joint, the end grain should be sized with glue. This is performed by applying a coat of thinned glue to the end grain, allowing it to air dry, and then recoating with unthinned glue. The parts are joined and clamped in the usual manner.

Fig. 3-42 Sizing end grain with glue.

When using cauls or blocks that cross the glue line, the work and block may be prevented from being glued to each other by using a piece of aluminum foil or wax paper between the two.

Fig. 3-43 Aluminum foil prevents cauls from being glued to the work.

Gluing Wide Boards

Gluing wide surfaces requires deep-throat clamps to reach the center of the assembly. If these are not available, a good substitute is curved cauls, which are made of hardwood and cut so that one long edge is slightly curved. In use, the curved edge is installed facing the work to be clamped. When pressure is applied to the outer edges of the cauls, an equal amount of pressure will occur at the center of the work.

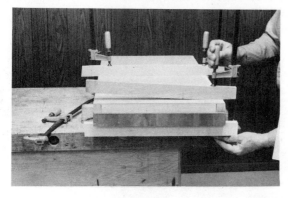

Fig. 3-44 Curved cauls substitute for deep clamps.

Wedges may be used to advantage when clamping boards. The longer the taper of the wedge, the better it will hold. If the use of wedges requires that the work being glued rest on a table or other surface, wax paper placed under the glue joint will prevent any squeeze-out from sticking to or damaging the surface.

Fig. 3-45 Using wedges to clamp a frame.

The frame-type parallelogram clamp should be made of stout lumber and lag bolts. Pressure is applied by striking the ends with a mallet.

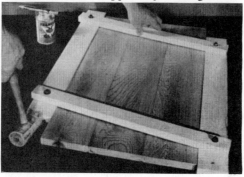

Fig. 3-46 A good substitute for clamps.

Pinch dogs may be used to pull joints together tightly. The wedge-shaped points are driven into the stock and then removed when the glue has set. The marks left in the wood may then be filled or plugged.

Fig. 3-47 Pinch dogs draw the joint tight.

Gluing Laminates

For cabinet work, plastic laminates should be bonded to a core material, such as particleboard or plywood. Particleboard is preferred for counters or tabletops because of its smooth surface. The heavy grain pattern of plywood may "telegraph" or show through the surface, especially when solid-color laminates without patterns are used. When surfaces to be laminated are unsupported—as is usually the case for tabletops—a backing material is used on the opposite side of the surface being laminated. The backing material is nondecorative and serves only as a moisture barrier, thus minimizing the possibility of warping.

Surfaces to be laminated must be clean and free of bumps, and all holes or voids must be filled. As mentioned previously, nonflammable adhesives are recommended, as is working in a well-ventilated area, preferably the outdoors. Although nonflammable adhesives will not burn or explode, the vapors are usually toxic, so caution must be used.

The cement is applied to the back of the laminate and to the face of the piece being covered with a brush, roller, or notched applicator. One pass over the surface is enough. Instructions for drying time should be followed.

Fig. 3-48 Applying cement to the laminate.

If the edges of the piece are to be laminated, they are glued and finished first. The top is generally the last piece to be applied.

Unlike wood glue, contact cement does not allow sliding or repositioning of the parts. Once the two surfaces are brought into contact, it is impossible to reposition them. The following procedure is therefore recommended. A coat of cement is applied to both surfaces and allowed to air dry until the surfaces no longer feel wet. This usually takes about forty-five minutes. Some wood surfaces may require two applications of cement. Next, two pieces of kraft wrapping paper are cut large enough to overhang the edges slightly and also to overlap near the center of the surface. They are then placed in position on the cemented surface. If the cement is properly dried, the paper will not stick to the surface. The laminate is positioned exactly over the paper. While the laminate is held in place, one end is carefully lifted and one of the kraft sheets gently removed. The laminate is pressed down lightly after the paper is removed. Then the other end of the laminate is lifted, and the balance of the paper is removed.

Another method of positioning the laminate makes use of dowels or sticks, which are placed on the work surface after the cement has set. The laminate is then positioned over the work, and, starting at one end, each stick is removed, one after the other, thus allowing the laminate to "fall" into place.

Fig. 3-49 Using sticks to align the laminate on cemented work.

When properly done, the laminate should overhang the work slightly all around.

Heavy pressure should now be applied to the surface with a small roller or wood block and hammer. Every square inch of surface is covered by rolling or hammering firmly.

When edge banding with laminate is required, it should be done before the top is applied. Usually, the edges are built up to give them a larger gluing area. The strips are added along the lower edge of the surface being laminated

Fig. 3-50 Applying pressure to the laminate with a small roller to concentrate the pressure.

and are applied with nails and glue and sanded smooth. If possible, the built-up strips should be 3/4 of an inch thick and from 1-1/2 to 2 inches wide. The edges must be perfectly aligned.

Since laminates must be trimmed flush after application, before adjacent pieces are added they must be applied in proper sequence. When edges, or sides, and a top are to be laminated, as in the case of a box, the following procedure should be used. With the box in the upright position, cement is applied to sides 1 and 3. Likewise, the appropriate pieces of laminate are coated. When the cement has set properly, side 3 is placed down on a clean sheet of kraft paper, and the laminate is applied to side 1, following the steps outlined above. Now the laminated side 1 is placed down on the kraft paper and side 3 is applied.

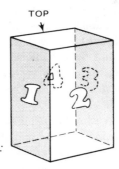

TOP

Fig. 3-51 The proper sequence for applying laminate: (1) sides 1 and 3; (2) sides 2 and 4; and (3) the top.

The overhang on both of these sides must now be trimmed with a router fitted with a straight laminate cutter. If a router is not available, a block plane is used, and the overhang is finished with a file. Sides 2 and 4 are done next in similar manner except for the trimming. The straight cutter is used along the top edges of sides 2 and 4, but the 22-1/2-degree beveling bit is used along the corners where sides 2 and 4 join sides 1 and 3. The top is added last, and the bevel cutter is used to trim all its edges. It should be noted that cement is applied in sections after a previous side or sides have been trimmed. If cement were applied to all surfaces at one time, the roller bearing of the cutter would make a mess of the cement. Also, the dust made by the cutter would adhere to the cemented surfaces.

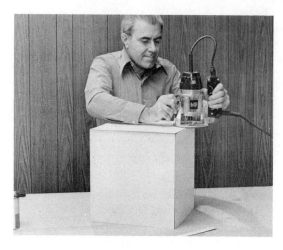

Fig. 3–52 Trimming overhang from the top.

BENDING WOOD

Curved surfaces in wood may be obtained by sawing or by bending. Sawing may not be practical, as end grain usually will cause weakness in the piece, and, additionally, sawing is usually very wasteful.

There are several ways to bend wood, including steaming, laminating, and kerfing. While steaming is not practical in the home shop, laminating and kerfing are. In laminating, two or more pieces of wood, with the grain direction running parallel, are glued in the bent shape. Bending forms are used to bend and hold the shaped wood after bending. Strips to be laminated must be thin and flexible enough to take the desired curve. As a rule, the sharper the curve, the thinner the strips must be. Allowance must be made for trimming laminated pieces, so the stock should always be cut larger than the finished size.

Fast-setting glues are not recommended for laminating work. The best all-around glue to use is the urea resin type. This is slow setting, does not stain, and is highly water resistant. If the laminated piece is to be used for outdoor construction, a completely waterproof resorcinol glue should be used. Knotted wood must never be used for bending, unless the knots occur on straight sections. The wood to be laminated must be cut into strips or sheets, and the necessary forms must be on hand and ready to use.

The bending forms must be rigid enough to withstand considerable pressure exerted by the work and the clamps. They must be smooth and free from defects; the curves must be smooth and free-flowing. Before applying glue, the parts should be assembled in a dry run to check the form. If the form is correct, the glue is applied to each piece, which is stacked until each piece has been coated. The inside and outside pieces should not be coated, and the worktable should be protected with wax paper or plastic sheeting. Clamping pressure is applied equally throughout the piece, and each clamp is tightened a little at a time. The glue must set thoroughly before the clamps are removed.

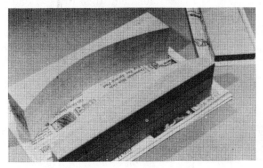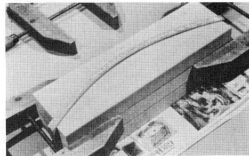

Fig. 3-53 Gluing jig for forming curved boards.

Kerfing is a method of bending wood by making a series of saw cuts side by side across the length of a piece of wood. The cuts are made close to the outside edge of the curved surface. Pieces bent by this method are very flexible but are rather weak unless supported. A strip of thin plywood or solid wood may be glued to the back side of the kerfed piece to reinforce it. Another method often used is to mix a paste of glue and sawdust which is then troweled into the grooves.

Fig. 3-54 Kerfing stock on the radial arm saw.

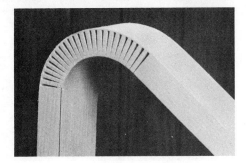

Fig. 3-55 A kerfed piece is easily bent into a sharp radius.

For most bending, the kerfs should be cut to within 1/16 of an inch of the curved surface. The spacing depends on the curve required. A simple way to determine the kerf spacing follows. A single kerf is cut in the wood to be curved. From this cut, a mark is placed on the stock equal to the radius required. The kerfed end of the board is clamped to the table, and then the free end is raised until the kerf closes. The distance from the table to the mark equals the kerf spacing. If the kerf cuts are made at an angle, the curved piece will assume a spiral shape. The pitch of the spiral will be equal to the angle of the kerf cuts.

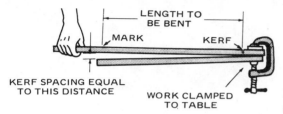

LENGTH TO
BE BENT

MARK   KERF

KERF SPACING EQUAL
TO THIS DISTANCE   WORK CLAMPED
TO TABLE

Fig. 3-56 A method of determining kerf spacing.

The kerfed piece may be mitered, rabbeted, or grooved, but these operations must be done before kerfing. Theoretically, a large radius or curve may be obtained simply by increasing the spacing between kerfs. This is not practical, however, because the result will be a series of flats instead of a smooth curve. To overcome this problem, either a thinner kerf should be used, or, if this is impractical, thickness should be added to the stock at the area to be curved.

Self-Bending

Some wood bending is referred to as "self-bending." This term relates to the bending of wood without steaming, laminating, or kerfing, and without the need for forming jigs. The wood normally used for this purpose is three-ply, one-eighth inch plywood, such as gum or bass. Plywood skins, which most lumberyards carry, are the facings used on hollow-core doors and measure three by seven feet. They are not as flexible as the gum, but they can be bent cold. The grain must run parallel to the bend, except for very slight bends which may be made across the grain.

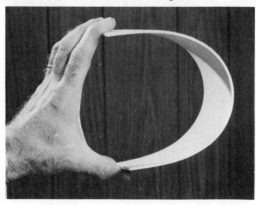

Fig. 3-57 Some plywood may be bent cold without forms.

EDGE TREATMENT

Although ideally suited for furniture construction, plywood has one major drawback: its edges are unsightly and must be concealed. One method often used for plywood shelves consists of a plastic bumper edging, which snaps into a groove cut in the plywood edge. Serrated projections on the tongue of the edging firmly grip the slot, thus eliminating the need for glue. This material may also be used for edges made with plastic laminates. When square edges are required, a thin veneer of the same type of wood may be used. This can be made in the shop, but it is far easier to purchase the veneer ready to use. The veneer is available as wood tape in rolls and is made a trifle wider than the edge to be covered. It is best applied with contact cement. Generally, because of the porosity of plywood edges, two coats of cement are required. After the tape has been applied and rolled firmly, it is trimmed with a sharp knife or razor blade and then sanded. The edges should be broken lightly with 6/0 paper.

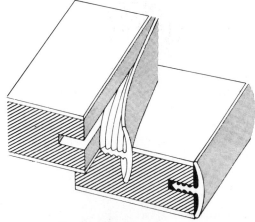

Fig. 3-58 Plastic edging snaps into place.

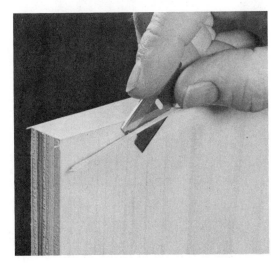

Fig. 3-59 Veneer edging is applied with contact cement and trimmed with a razor blade.

Solid wood may also be used for edging. The edging is ripped from solid stock and fastened with glue and brads which should be set below the surface. The use of clamps eliminates the need for brads. Flat-wood edging may also be installed with splines, tongue and groove, or V-joints.

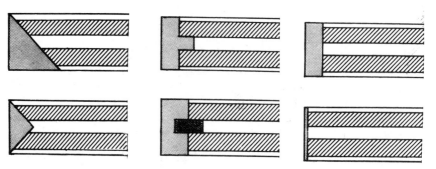

Fig. 3-60 Various edge treatments for plywood.

The solid-wood edging may be shaped for a decorative effect. This is often done on tabletops. The edge may be the same thickness as the top or, for a heavier look, the edging may be made of thicker stock. The edges may be shaped before or after installation. Usually the shaping is done afterwards, as it is easier to clamp square-edged stock to the panel. Sometimes a narrow kerf cut is made at the edge of the plywood to form a separation between it and the edge. This eliminates the need for a perfect match between the plywood and the solid edging. This method is also used when laminate and wood edging are combined.

Fig. 3-61 When molding is applied to a top, it should be set a trifle below the surface.

KERF

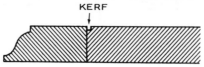

Fig. 3-62 Shallow kerf forms a gap between edging and top.

FASTENING METHODS

Various fasteners are used in furniture construction, including nails, screws, dowels, bolts, splines, and others.

Nails

Nails do not have the holding power of screws but are commonly used when exceptional holding power is not needed. Nails come in many sizes and styles. For cabinetry, the most often used are casing and finishing nails. Casing nails have a conical head and hold better than finishing nails, which have a smaller head.

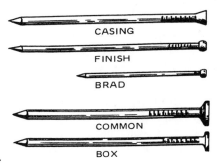

Fig. 3-63 Various nail types.

Nails are designated in inch or penny size. In the past, *penny* referred to the price of various sized nails per hundred. It now refers to the length of the nail and is expressed by the small letter *d* following a numeral, such as 4d, 6d, etc. Each penny increase means a quarter-inch increase in the length of the nail. A 2d nail is one inch long; a 4d nail is 1-1/2 inches long, etc.

The length of a nail should be at least three times the thickness of the material being fastened, with a few exceptions. For better holding power, nails should be driven at a slight angle to each other. For greater holding power, annular or spiral shank nails are used. Flat-headed nails should be driven flush. Casing and finishing nails are driven so that the head protrudes slightly; they are then driven slightly below the surface with a nail set, which prevents hammer marks on the surface.

If there is a possibility of the wood splitting when driving nails close to an end of the board, the point of the nail should be blunted slightly to prevent splitting. When driving nails into hardwoods, it may be necessary to drill a pilot hole slightly smaller in diameter than the nail size.

When using a glue and nail combination, before applying the glue a few nails are started through the first piece and only partially into the second. This locates the parts. The nails are then withdrawn from the second piece, the glue applied, the protruding nails reinserted into the nail holes, and the nailing completed.

Screws

Having far greater holding power than nails, screws are made in various metals and shapes. Flat- and round-head screws are the most commonly used in the home shop. For greater strength and holding power, lag screws and lag bolts are often used. These have square or hexagonal heads which are driven with a wrench.

Fig. 3-64 Lag screw.

Wood screws are identified by length, gauge, and head type. Thus, 1-1/4–8 FH indicates a 1-1/4-inch-long screw which is 8 gauge in diameter with a flat head. Each gauge rating increases or decreases by 13/1000 (.013) of an inch. Screws should penetrate the second block by at least two-thirds of their length.

To properly drive a screw, it is necessary to bore two holes: one for the shank (threadless part), and one for the threaded part. These are called shank and pilot holes. The shank hole should be a trifle larger than the shank diameter, and the screw should fit the hole freely. The pilot hole is made just a trifle smaller than the root diameter of the screw: for hardwoods, about 10 percent smaller, and for softwoods about 30 percent smaller. When penetrating hardwoods, it is sometimes helpful to lubricate the threads of the screw with soap or wax. This is especially important when the screws are brass or bronze, as they can easily break.

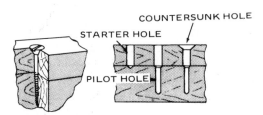

COUNTERSUNK HOLE

STARTER HOLE

PILOT HOLE

Fig. 3-65 The proper method of sinking a screw.

Plugs and Buttons

When using flat-head screws, the hole should be countersunk so that the head is flush with the work surface. If plugs or buttons are to be used to conceal the screw heads, the hole is counterbored to a depth of 1/4 to 5/16 of an inch. Buttons are decorative and installed protruding from the surface.

Wood plugs are installed flush with the surface. They should be cut from the same species of wood as is used in the furniture piece, unless a contrasting effect is desired. Plugs are made with a plug cutter, as explained earlier.

When installing buttons or plugs, glue should not be applied to either. Instead, glue should be applied to the walls of the hole with a small brush. If glue is spread on the plug, most of it will scrape off the sides and get onto the work surface. This may cause problems later when staining the piece.

Fig. 3-66 Decorative buttons conceal the screw heads.

Fig. 3-67 Plugging screw head holes.

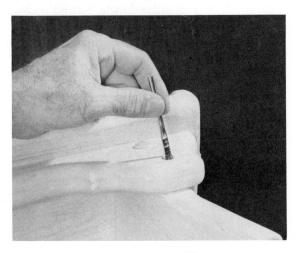

Fig. 3-68 Glue should be applied to the hole to prevent oozing.

*Fig. 3-69 Glue ooze will cause prob-
lems when finishing a piece.*

Bolts

Hanger bolts are useful for mounting legs and reinforcing blocks. They have a wood screw at one end and a machine screw at the opposite end. The pointed end is driven into one member of the furniture. The machine end is threaded onto a mounting plate, or, in the case of the reinforcing block, it is passed through the block which is then held with a washer and nut. Dowel screws are similar but have a pointed wood screw at each end.

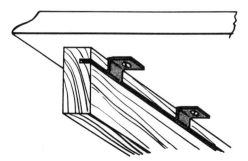

*Fig. 3-70 Top—hanger bolt; bottom—
dowel screw.*

Tabletops must be fastened from the underside, except when plugs are permissible, in which case they may be attached with screws and plugged. Blind fastening methods include cleats, diagonal screws, and top fasteners—both metal and wood. If a top is made of solid lumber, provision must be made for expansion and contraction. Failure to provide for such movement will cause problems in the finished piece. Buckling or cracking of the wood members will result,

*Fig. 3-71 Metal tabletop
fasteners.*

especially if the members are wide. For solid tops, the wood or metal type fasteners are recommended, as they will permit expansion and contraction movement. Whether wood blocks or metal fasteners are used, they should be installed so the end is just short of the dado or groove. Professionals usually use the metal fasteners.

Cleats, angle brackets, and diagonally mounted screws are recommended when the tops are made of plywood, particleboard, or other stable materials which are not subject to expansion and contraction. When solid lumber members are to be fastened, allowance must be provided for movement of the parts. This is normally done by enlarging the shank holes in the cleats or other members.

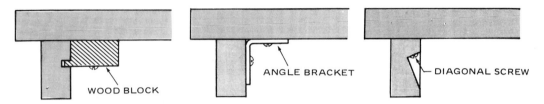

WOOD BLOCK   ANGLE BRACKET   DIAGONAL SCREW

Fig. 3-72 Three additional methods of fastening tops.

Another method of fastening tops utilizes a subtop. This consists of a strip of wood, at the front and rear of the case, fastened to cleats at each end. The top is then fastened to the subtop from the underside.

Other methods of fastening make use of knock-down fasteners, rail fasteners, tee nuts, threaded inserts, and flush-mount hangers. The knock-down fastener is useful for assembling parts which may be taken apart and reassembled whenever the need arises. The interlocking parts are made in pairs and are easy to use.

Rail fasteners are used mainly for fastening the rails of beds to corner posts. Made of heavy steel, they consist of swaged hooks which engage a slot in the mating element. Another type of fastener is made with tapering sections, which are also useful for hanging flush fixtures. Threaded inserts permit the use of machine screws and bolts in wood. They are also useful for assembling parts to particleboard. A hole is bored into the wood the same size as the root diameter of the insert. A slot at one end of the insert permits the use of a screwdriver to drive it home.

Fig. 3-73 Threaded insert for wood.

Chapter 4

FURNITURE
CONSTRUCTION

A basic study of furniture construction not only will aid the woodworker to build good furniture, but also will assist any buyer of ready-made furniture to make a much wiser selection. The buyer will recognize furniture to be of high quality when the interiors—although not as finely finished as the exteriors— are at least sanded and stained or waxed. He will note if nail heads have been countersunk and concealed. He will look for dovetail joints in drawers and note whether drawer sides have been sanded smooth and waxed. Dustproof panels between drawers are also a clue to high-quality construction. Back panels should be sanded smooth, stained, and properly supported along the bottom. If cabinet backs are glued as well as screwed or nailed, it means better insurance against dust, mold, and moths. These are only some of the important features of good furniture construction. It is hoped that the reader—whether experienced woodworker, student or consumer— will benefit by this book and learn to recognize and build well-constructed furniture.

Furniture may be made of solid stock or with frame-and-panel construction. Warping is always a problem with solid-stock construction, even when such man-made materials as plywood or particleboard are used. This is not so with frame-and-panel construction. High stability, even in conditions of considerable humidity, is its chief advantage. Another favorable feature is the weight factor: framed panels are much lighter than those of solid construction. Not all furniture lends itself to panel construction, however. Some pieces may be made entirely of framed panels, others may be of solid construction with the exception of framed doors, while others are more suited to solid construction. This is especially true of pine furniture, which is often made of solid stock, although framed doors may be included.

Fig. 4-1 A dry sink/hutch made of solid pine.

In frame construction, the vertical members are called the stiles, and the horizontal members are known as the rails. If the frame is to receive a wood panel, the inner edge is usually grooved to take the panel, thus locking it in permanently. If glass is used, the inner edge of the frame is rabbeted so that the glass may be replaced if necessary. In some designs, the panel is set flush, in which case a rabbet is cut at the front inner edge of the frame members.

Fig. 4-2 A typical frame construction. The doors are framed to take glass.

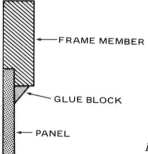

FRAME MEMBER

GLUE BLOCK

PANEL

Fig. 4-3 The section through the frame is rabbeted to hold a flush panel.

Frames are also used in cabinets as drawer supports. In quality furniture, these may be fitted with dust panels, thus preventing dust from the drawers above from settling on the lower drawers. The frames also add stability to the pieces. The joints used to assemble the frame may be doweled, mortised and tenoned, or simply butted.

Fig. 4-4 A rear view of framed drawer supports and drawers.

The use of solid stock greatly simplifies construction, and, thanks to plywood and other available materials, production time is considerably reduced. True, plywood will be affected by humidity, but the effect is minimal, except when large pieces are involved.

Since solid lumber is least stable across the grain, care should be taken that the grain runs in the proper direction among the parts of the assembly.

Fig. 4-5 Grain direction is important when pieces are made of solid lumber.

Basically, the building of furniture requires the construction of a box that may be fitted with doors, drawers, and shelves. Legs may be added to the piece or may be an integral part of it.

Some furniture pieces are made with top, sides, and bottom joined with miters at the corners; others may be made with the top and bottom overlapping the sides; and, although not too common, sides may be made to overlap the top and bottom. The joints used for overlapping sections may be doweled, dadoed, splined, or mortised and tenoned.

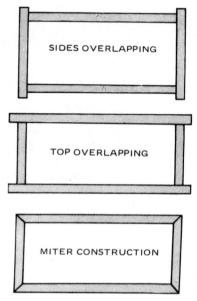

SIDES OVERLAPPING

TOP OVERLAPPING

MITER CONSTRUCTION

Fig. 4-6 A front view of three types of furniture construction.

Large pieces may require the construction of separate sections which are then combined. A typical piece may consist of a base, lower cabinet, upper cabinet, and cornice. The base unit may consist of legs attached directly to the lower cabinet; legs and rail assembled as a unit; or a plinth or pedestal, which may be a rectangular frame, plain or fancy. The base unit is usually fastened by means of cleats. Corner blocks may be added for rigidity.

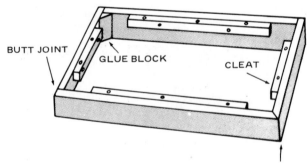

BUTT JOINT

GLUE BLOCK   CLEAT

MITER JOINT   *Fig. 4-7 A typical cabinet base.*

The lower cabinet may contain doors, drawers, shelves, partitions, or dividers. The upper cabinet is usually made with shelves and doors and may be topped with a decorative molding or cornice.

The internal framing of a case may be made of solid plywood, but this adds to the weight and cost. A more practical approach is to use the web frame. The end panels are usually dadoed to receive the web frame. The dadoes are then cut with a router or on the table saw. It is recommended to make a test cut on scrap wood to check the width and depth of the dado.

Fig. 4-8 Dadoing end panels of a cabinet with a router.

The usual practice is to make the frames slightly oversize, then to trim them to size after gluing. The trimming operation eliminates the need to use cauls when clamping and also makes for greater accuracy. When all of the parts have been made and trimmed, they should be assembled dry to make certain each piece fits properly. If the end panels are made of plywood, the frames may be glued. If the end panels are constructed of solid lumber, the frames may be glued only if the grain direction of the frame is parallel to that of the end panel.

Fig. 4-9 The cauls under clamps may be eliminated if frame members are made slightly oversize.

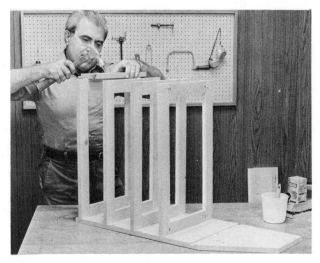

Fig. 4-10 Dry fitting parts to test the fit.

The simplest joint for assembling the web frame to a vertical member is the butt joint, which is assembled either with screws or nails from the outside, or with cleats on the inside. If the piece is to be laminated, the nail and screw heads will not matter. For exposed surfaces, fastener heads must be concealed with filler, buttons, or plugs. The dado and rabbeted dado are superior to the butt joint. Stopped dadoes should be used when the front edge of the piece is exposed. If a face frame or lamination is to be used, the dadoes may run to the edge. Shortened dadoes should stop about one-half of an inch from the edge.

Fig. 4-11 These frame members are fastened to the sides with screws.

The usual procedure for installing rear panels is to set them into a rabbet cut into the rear of the piece. The rabbet should be the same depth as the rear panel, or slightly deeper. If the piece is to be installed against a wall, such as a kitchen cabinet, the rear panel should be set in about one-half of an inch to allow for trimming the piece to fit discrepancies in the wall.

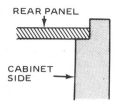

REAR PANEL

CABINET
SIDE

Fig. 4-12 The deep-set rear panel is recommended for wall-mounted cabinets.

DRAWER CONSTRUCTION

Drawers are of two basic types: flush or overlap. The flush drawer requires greater accuracy in construction and fitting since any discrepancies between the frame and drawer edge are clearly visible. In overlapping drawers, the space between the drawer sides and frame is concealed.

Fig. 4-13 Left—flush drawer; right—overlapping drawer.

Drawers have five component parts: front, rear, sides, and bottom. Joints may vary in different drawers, but the basic drawer is shown in Figure 4-14.

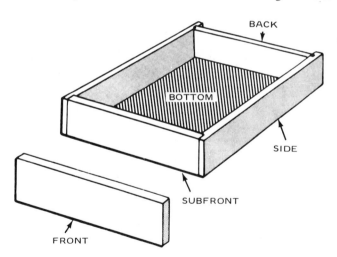

Fig. 4-14 The component parts of a drawer.

Drawer fronts are usually made of 3/4-inch stock, but 1-1/8-inch fronts are not uncommon. The fronts may be made of solid lumber, lumber core plywood, or veneer core plywood. In some construction, a solid lumber front is added to the basic drawer. In such drawers, the parts are referred to as the front and the subfront. The fronts may be decorated in various ways—raised, carved, laminated, or appliqued. Moldings also may be added.

Fig. 4-15 A drawer construction showing the front and subfront.

Fig. 4-16 Drawer fronts being decorated with moldings.

The sides of drawers are usually made of 1/2-inch stock. Small drawers may be made of 3/8-inch material, and, if side guides are used, 3/4-inch material may be necessary. Solid wood and plywood are both used in construction. In quality work, the sides are generally made of hardwood, and the top edges are rounded. Grooves are cut near the lower edge to receive the drawer bottom.

Fig. 4-17 A drawer front being fastened to its sides.

Drawer backs are generally made of 1/2-inch stock. They may be grooved as the side and front panels, or they may simply rest on the bottom panel. In better construction they are always grooved.

The standard for drawer bottoms is 1/4-inch material, either plywood or hardboard. They are cut to fit with a 1/32-inch clearance all around. If the back panel is not grooved, nails or staples are used to fasten the bottom to the underside of the rear panel. Glue must *never* be used to hold the bottom panel. Only nails should be used at the rear, or, if the back panel is grooved, nails are not required. Glue blocks may be used, however, for extra support. These are placed at intervals along the bottom at the front, sides, and rear. In simple construction, the drawer bottom may be nailed to the sides, front, and back.

Fig. 4-18 Drawer bottoms are installed without glue.

DRAWER JOINTS

The joints used in drawer construction depend on the equipment available and the degree of quality required. The multiple dovetail joint is found on high-quality furniture. Although this joint may be constructed by hand, it is generally made with a router and special dovetail template. The device is designed to hold and cut both members of the drawer at the same time. The attachment should be screwed or clamped to the workbench. Then the work is clamped with the inner face of the drawer side facing outward. If properly done, the parts will

Fig. 4-19 A surface-mounted drawer bottom.

fit perfectly. The various joints used in drawer construction are shown in Figure 4-22. Drawers should be made after the cabinet is completed; thus, if there are any discrepancies, the drawers may be fitted accordingly.

Fig. 4-20 Using a template to cut multiple dovetails in drawer parts.

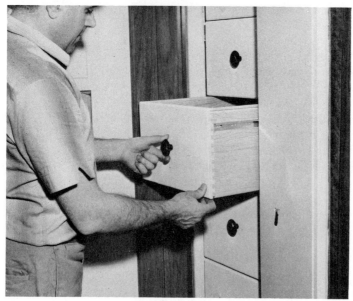

Fig. 4-21 A completed drawer with dovetail joints.

The drawer size depends in part on the type of guides used. Guides are the runners or tracks on which the drawers ride. There are three basic types: side-, corner-, and center-mounted guides.

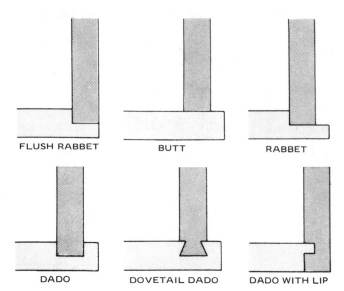

FLUSH RABBET   BUTT   RABBET

DADO   DOVETAIL DADO   DADO WITH LIP

Fig. 4-22 Various joints used for the front and side members of drawers.

In the side guide type, grooves are cut in the drawer side panels. They are usually placed slightly above center. Hardwood strips are then fastened to both sides of the cabinet interior so the drawer may ride on them. In another version, the grooves are cut in the cabinet sides and the strips are added to the drawer sides. Both versions work equally well, but the grooved drawer type is more often used, as it is easier to make the grooves in the smaller drawer sections rather than in the larger cabinet sides.

The corner guide has an L-shaped strip which supports the bottom and sides of the drawer.

The center guide utilizes a grooved wood strip attached to the center of the drawer bottom. It rides on a runner which is attached to the framing. On very wide drawers, two guides may be used instead of a single center one. The center and side guide drawers usually require a kicker, which is a strip of wood fastened to the cabinet above each drawer. The kicker prevents the drawer from tipping downward when extended.

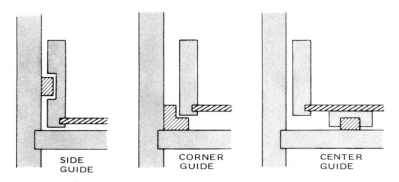

SIDE GUIDE   CORNER GUIDE   CENTER GUIDE

Fig. 4-23 Three methods of guiding a drawer.

Fig. 4-24 Installing a center wood guide to a drawer bottom.

Commercial guides and slides are also available. These operate at the sides or bottom of drawers. Most have stops to limit the amount the drawer will extend. Some have self-closing features.

Drawers are often separated into sections or compartments. In high-quality work, dadoes are cut into the sides or front and rear panels. Dividers are then cut and fitted into the dadoes. In a simpler method, plastic divider supports are installed. Some of these have sharp barbs molded into the rear edge, and they are simply pressed into place and will hold the divider snugly.

FRAME-AND-PANEL CONSTRUCTION

Frame-and-panel construction is widely used in furniture construction because of the many advantages it offers. Among its benefits are dimensional stability, warp resistance, styling, lighter weight, and usually lower cost. Few commercially made pieces (except for pine) are made entirely of solid stock. Most pieces have frame-and-panel doors, and in many others the sides and top may be made this way.

The basic parts of the frame-and-panel consist of the stiles, rails, and panel. The stiles are the two vertical members; the rails are the horizontal members and run across the top and bottom; and the panel fits within the assembled stiles and rails.

Intermediate stiles are called cross-stiles or mullions, and the intermediate rails are called cross-rails. The frame (stiles and rails) is made of solid lumber, but the panel may consist of plywood or solid glued-up stock. Corner joints for the frame vary, but the most popular—especially for the home craftsman— are the dowel and stub tenon.

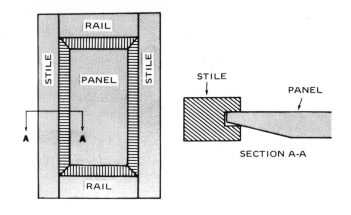

Fig. 4-25 Parts of the frame and panel.

The panel fits into a groove or rabbet cut into the frame. Usually the groove cut in the rails is three-eighths of an inch deep, but in the stiles, the depth must be greater (about one-half of an inch), especially if solid lumber panels are used. The extra depth in the stiles will allow for the greater cross-grain expansion of the panel. Rather than make two different depths, the groove is usually cut to the deeper dimension all around.

The panel is never glued into place. This would prevent movement during expansion and contraction of the parts and could result in warpage or worse, such as split joints in the frame or panel.

Raised panels may be shouldered or beveled using a table saw, radial arm saw, or shaper. If the panel has an irregular outline, the shaper must be used. When using the table saw to make a raised panel, the blade is elevated to the desired height. If the raise is to be beveled, the saw arbor is tilted accordingly. The cross-grain cuts are made first. The with-the-grain cuts are made last and will remove any splintering. When thin stock is being raised, it may be necessary to clamp a piece of wood to the work. The wood is made to "ride" the fence, thus preventing the work from dropping into the table cutout.

Fig. 4-26 A stub tenon joint.

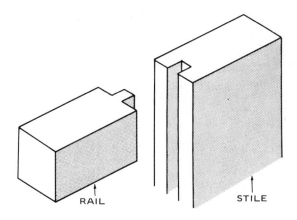

Door panels with molded edges require the use of a shaper with a matched set of sticking cutters to make cove and bead cuts on the inside edge of the stiles and rails and to make the cope cut at the rail ends. Since such equipment is not usually found in the home shop, a simpler method may be used to produce similar results. In one method, the frame is made in the usual manner with the appropriate groove for the panel. Stopped grooves are made in the stiles. The frame members are then assembled dry, and a router is used to shape the edges. It may be necessary to insert a temporary filler strip in the groove to provide a surface for the router bit pilot. When shaping is done, the frame is disassembled, glue applied to the joints, the panel installed, and the frame clamped. The corners of the shaped edges will have a slight radius which has a pleasing appearance. This method may be used on straight or irregular frames. If sharp corners are desired, this may be done with a chisel and careful trimming.

Fig. 4-27 Raised panels made on the table saw.

Another method utilizes applied moldings to give the effect of a panel. A pleasing raised panel effect may be achieved by using appliqués shaped with a router. Rectangular- or irregular-shaped pieces are cut to the required size and shaped. These are then fastened to the panel, which in turn is mounted into the frame. The appliqués may be applied singly or in multiples.

Fig. 4-28 Using the router to shape a door panel.

Fig. 4-29 Using moldings for a panel effect on doors.

Flush panels are usually used for cabinet sides. These are set into a rabbet cut into the frame edge, or the panel edge may be rabbeted to set into a groove cut in the frame.

FURNITURE DOORS

There are two general types of doors used in furniture: swinging and sliding. In both groups, there are such kinds as solid, panel-and-frame, frame-and-skin, frame-and-grille, glass, tambour, and bypass. Solid lumber doors should be used only when the size is relatively small because they have a tendency to warp and their size is affected by temperature and humidity. Lumber core and plywood doors, however, are stable and highly suited for use on furniture and built-ins.

Swinging or hinged doors may be flush, lipped, or have a full overlap.

Fig. 4-30 A raised panel effect achieved with appliqués.

Lipped doors are easier to fit than flush doors because they cover part of the face frame. Flush doors, however, must be fitted into the framework so that all surfaces are level. The full overlap door covers all edges of the frame and is generally used in contemporary type furniture.

When flush doors meet without a post or stile between them, some means must be used to eliminate the opening which results because of the space between them. Several methods of solving this problem are possible. One is to fasten a strip of wood to the back side of one door. The strip is made to overhang the edge and thus serves as a stop. Another method utilizes a rabbet joint along the meeting edges of both doors. Often to improve the appearance of the piece, a bead or raised edge is added to one of the doors. This will make the separation of the doors distinct.

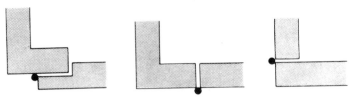

Fig. 4-31 Hinged-type doors: left—overlapping; center—flush; right—full overlap.

Wood, plastic, glass, and hardboard are most commonly used in constructing sliding doors. The doors slide in grooves cut in the cabinet frame or in tracks mounted on the edge of the frame. The tracks may be factory-made or home-made with square strips and quarter-round molding. The square strips are used between the doors, and the quarter-round molding is placed at the front and rear of the doors, parallel to the narrow strip to form a groove or track. The upper grooves for the sliding doors are deeper than the lower ones; the lower ones are usually three-sixteenths of an inch deep, the upper three-eighths of an inch deep. The doors are installed by pushing them upwards so the top edges enter into the upper grooves first; then the doors are lowered so that the bottom edges drop into the lower track.

Fig. 4-32 The piece at the left utilizes sliding doors.

A disadvantage of sliding doors is that only 50 percent of the cabinet is accessible at any time. To overcome this, tambour doors may be used. These are flexible and may be made to slide around corners so that the door becomes invisible. The easiest way to make these doors is to glue a canvas to the back side of wood strips. The ends of the strips are notched to fit over a flexible plastic track. Tambour doors may also be constructed to ride in grooves cut in the cabinet members. The ends of the slats or strips are not notched when this method is used. Rolltop desks are usually made this way.

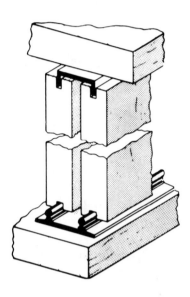

Fig. 4-33 Sliding doors riding on a plastic track.

HANGING DOORS

Various types of hinges may be used for hanging doors, but the butt hinge is the most common, especially for flush doors. The door must be carefully fitted and, if necessary, it should be trimmed so it fits the opening with 1/32 of an inch clearance all around. The usual procedure followed for marking the hinge location is to wedge the door in the opening while marking the hinge position on the door and frame. A better method follows.

The hinges are first located and installed on the door. No gain need be cut for nonmortise hinges. After the hinges are installed on the door, the door is placed with hinges extended into the opening and wedged at the top and bottom so it is centered. The position of each hinge is marked lightly on the frame with a pencil. A duplicate hinge is positioned on the frame between the pencil lines and set backwards on the frame with the knuckle up against the front of the frame. The screw hole locations are now marked, and pilots for the screws are drilled. This procedure is repeated for the other hinges and then the hinges are attached permanently. This is one of the most accurate methods of installing hinges and it is highly recommended.

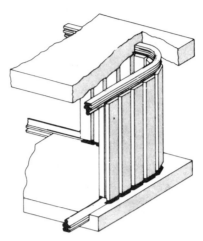

Fig. 4-34 A flexible plastic track is used to guide tambour doors. The cabinet must be grooved to take the track.

If mortise type hinges are used, the gain must be cut in the door and frame before installing the hinges. It should be noted that the gain may be cut one-half in the frame and one-half in the door, but it is far easier to cut the total gain in the door only. One leaf of the hinge is then surface mounted on the frame.

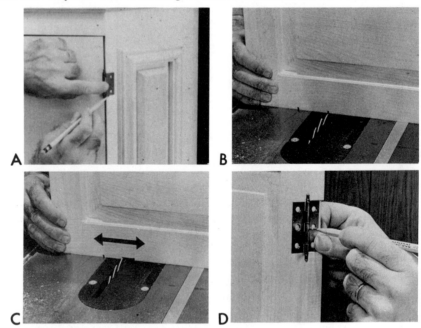

Fig. 4-35 Steps in hanging a cabinet door:
  A. The hinge position is marked on the door and frame.
  B. Set the blade to protrude the depth of the mortise, then support the work against miter gauge and make outer cuts.
  C. Slowly slide the piece from left to right as indicated by the arrow, advancing the miter gauge slightly after each pass.
  D. Holding the hinge in place, mark the screw holes. Then make a pilot hole and fasten with screws.

Chapter 5

HARDWARE

Hardware is used in practically all furniture construction, and, without question, it is important to select the proper type and style depending on whether its use is mainly functional or decorative. A heavy door supported by fragile small hinges will eventually sag or drop off. A contemporary chest will look odd if early American pulls or knobs are installed on the drawers. There is a wide range of hardware available, including hinges, pulls, knobs, casters, and specialty hardware. Therefore, one should have no trouble finding the right piece of hardware for a project. Regardless of the type of hardware selected, it should be on hand before a project is started so that proper clearances and allowances may be made during construction.

Drop-leaf supports are used with hinges to support leaves of tables, shelves, and doors. They are often used with piano or continuous hinges. Some supports are spring loaded and will lock securely in place. Others are hinged and swing flush against the cabinet side when the leaf is down.

Fig. 5-1 Drop leaf support.

Lids for desks require pivot knife hinges and some type of support, such as a chain or flap stay. Lids on stereos, bars, phonographs, and similar furniture in which the lid must be raised and held in a vertical position require the use of

Fig. 5-2 Single-slide lid support.

lift-up supports. Some are made to lock in opening and unlock in closing. The better ones are made to close slowly after release.

Fig. 5-3 Spring-loaded, self-balancing lid support.

Pulls for doors and drawers are made in a multitude of styles, sizes, and materials. The type used will depend on the style of the furniture piece. When numerous drawer fronts or doors must have duplicate holes bored for the installation of the same pulls, the use of a simple jig will speed up the task. In industry, such jigs are made with steel bushings so that they will last. However, for the home craftsman, a simple board with the necessary holes drilled at the proper spacing will suffice. A stop nailed to the top and one end of the board will ensure that the holes are properly located.

For small doors and drawers, it is customary to use knobs instead of pulls. The knobs are available in glass, bright brass, chrome, pewter, ceramic, and, of course, wood. Sometimes they are furnished with a backplate, which is decorative and also protects against fingerprints.

Metal ornaments are often used on furniture. Campaign corners and pulls are very popular. They are generally installed with matching escutcheon pins. Stars and eagle ornaments are traditional for early American pieces. Most metallic

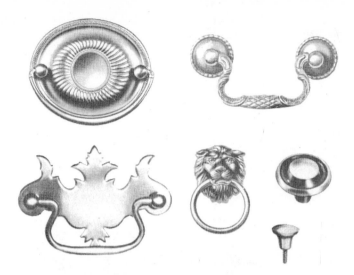

Fig. 5-4 Cabinet pulls.

Fig. 5-5 Simple jig speeds up hole
boring job for identical drawer pulls.

ornaments are given a protective coat of lacquer to preserve the surface, whether it be solid or plated. It is important that abrasive cleaners or steel wool never be used on these, as once the coating is removed, the pieces will tarnish.

HINGES

Made in many styles for various applications, most hinges are metal, but plastic hinges are also made. Some hinges are made with loose pins, and these must be installed with the pin "up." Most hinges, however, are of the fixed-pin type which may be used upright or upside down. Some of the more common hinges and their uses are described below.

Strip or piano hinges are made in long lengths—usually six feet—and are used on doors or lids which require full support. These hinges have countersunk holes for flathead or oval-head screws. Of the two, the oval-head screw will have a better appearance. The material used for these hinges is very thin, and if the flathead screw is not perfectly centered, it will not seat properly and its appearance will be unsightly. If brass screws are used, it is recommended to form the screw hole with a steel screw first, then to replace it with the brass screw. This will prevent screw breakage, which can ruin a job. (This advice applies to all brass screw installations.)

Saw-kerf hinges made of plastic are applied without screws. A barbed strip is inserted in a kerf cut into the door and cabinet case.

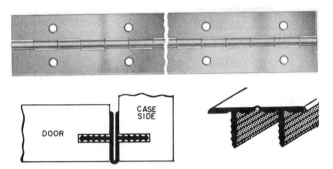

Fig. 5-6 Top—metal strip hinge; bottom—saw kerf plastic hinge.

Butt hinges are made in mortise and nonmortise styles. Some have finials for a decorative effect. For flush door applications with mortise-type hinges, a 1/32 of an inch clearance is used between door and frame. When nonmortise hinges are used, the clearance on the hinge side should be equal to the thickness of the hinge.

Fig. 5-7 Typical butt hinge mortised into case side.

Concealed hinges—also known as pin hinges—are made in many configurations. They permit doors to open 180 degrees, and some are made so that the door will swing around to the sides a full 240 degrees. When the door is closed, the only part showing on these hinges is the pin.

Fig. 5–8 Concealed hinge.

Double-bend hinges are used for lay-on doors. Since only the knuckle shows on these, they are often used for clock doors and small cabinets.

Fig. 5–9 Nonmortise, double-bend hinge.

Flip-top hinges are used on tables where the top must swing 180 degrees, as in a bar-top table or server. These hinges are usually made of polished brass and used on better-quality furniture.

Butler-tray hinges are used on butler-tray tables. They support the flaps of the table at any angle from zero to ninety degrees. The better ones are spring loaded, which accounts for their rather high cost.

Fig. 5–10 Spring-loaded butler tray hinge. This one has tension adjustment.

Drawer slides, commercially made, are side, top, or bottom mounted. The top-mounted slides are useful when it is impractical to mount the guides at the side or bottom of a drawer. Some drawer slides are made entirely of plastic. The advantages of the plastic ones are their low cost and quiet operation, and they can be stapled to the drawers and case sides.

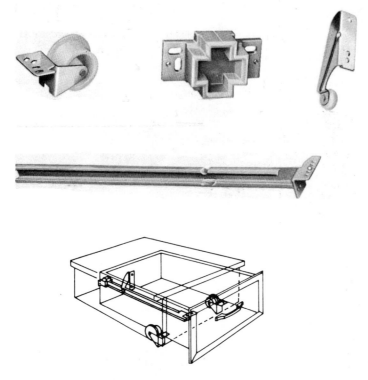

Fig. 5-11 Commercial drawer slide hardware.

CATCHES

Various catches for holding doors closed are available, the most popular being the magnetic catch. Magnetic catches are made in many styles. Some are attached to the frame with screws, while others are pressed into holes bored in the edge of the cabinet. The keepers are usually mounted to the doors. Some catches are made with adjustable magnets which permit very fine adjustment.

Fig. 5-12 Magnetic door catch.

The size of the magnetic catch used depends on its application. Too strong a magnet may hold too well. This would be objectionable on some furniture, especially tall clocks and curio cabinets, since they could be tipped over if the catch did not yield easily.

Friction and roller catches are also used on furniture cabinets. On some, the tension may be adjusted to provide positive locking and easy opening.

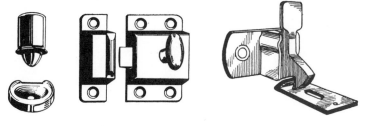

Fig. 5-13 Typical cabinet catches: bullet, cupboard, elbow.

Touch latches are unique in that they eliminate the need for handles or pulls on cabinet doors. They close and open doors automatically at a slight touch. Spring loaded, they are completely concealed from exterior view.

Swivel casters are often attached to the base of heavy pieces of furniture to give the furniture easy mobility without marring the floor or carpeting underneath. They may be found on large beds, double dressers, armoires, etc. The casters may be ball-shaped, flat rollers, or wheels. Concealed casters are useful for heavy furniture. Some have self-aligning brackets which simplify installation.

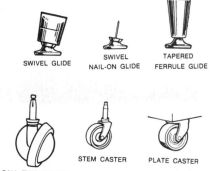

SWIVEL GLIDE   SWIVEL NAIL-ON GLIDE   TAPERED FERRULE GLIDE

STEM CASTER   PLATE CASTER

Fig. 5-14 Furniture glides and casters. BALL TYPE CASTER

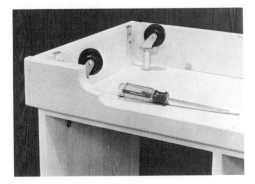

Fig. 5-15 Concealed casters.

Chapter 6

FURNITURE FINISHING

The finishing operation will affect many factors in the final appearance of the wood, such as color, depth, graining, and sheen. Therefore, it is an extremely important process for all styles of furniture. Undoubtedly finishing is time-consuming, but it represents time well spent. The finisher must know the qualities of the wood he is working with and the proper finish to use to obtain the desired result. This skill is acquired only by a great deal of practice.

A fine woodworking project may be spoiled by a poor or mediocre finish. This is unfortunate, because there is no good reason for such a failure. Using modern technology and the vast array of finishing materials avaiable, even a novice should be able to turn out a fine finish. It is important that certain basic rules and procedures be followed. One of the greatest causes of failure is due to impatience on the part of the worker. Some stages of finishing cannot be rushed. If instructions call for overnight drying, they mean just that. For example, solvents must evaporate completely from fillers; otherwise, they will be trapped under succeeding topcoats, forming a milky appearance. Many other problems are caused by improper drying or poor sanding. Humidity may also cause finishing problems. Moisture trapped in a finish will cause blooming and other defects.

Another pitfall encountered by the novice is misinformation. If ten people are asked how to finish a piece of wood, chances are ten different answers will be offered. This is not to imply that there is only one way to produce a finish. Many variations are possible to produce the same end result, but certain basic techniques are essential.

Furniture may be finished with opaque or clear finishes. Oil paints, colored lacquers, latex paints, and epoxies all produce an opaque finish. Clear finishes include transparent stains, varnish, lacquer, shellac, oil, wax, and others. Opaque finishes conceal the grain pattern of the wood and are seldom used on fine

117

furniture. There is one exception however, and 'this is in the art of antiquing, which utilizes opaque paints with other materials. Antiquing is widely used today on old and new furniture alike.

PREPARING THE WORK

To produce a fine finish, the work must be free of defects and smooth. Finishing will not conceal defects or rough sanding marks. In most cases, the finish will intensify them. Therefore, any defects in the wood—such as dents, cracks, and holes—must be attended to before finish sanding.

If the wood has been dented slightly, a damp cloth heated over the spot will usually suffice to remove the dent. If a hot iron is placed on the cloth and held there momentarily, the steam from the cloth will swell the wood to its original form. If necessary, this may be repeated several times, but care must be taken to avoid scorching the wood.

Fig. 6-1 Steaming a shallow dent.

Cracks and holes may be corrected in several ways. Small cracks and holes may be filled with such materials as wood dough, wood putty, plastic wood, etc. Some are premixed and ready to use; others must be mixed with water before application. If the furniture piece is to be finished with an opaque medium, the color of the filler will not matter. For stained work, however, the filler should have the same color as the stain. Some fillers are available in various wood tones; others are white or cream colored and must be tinted before use. One type of wood putty which is made in powder form may be mixed with dry colors available at all paint shops. The fillers above are not to be confused with paste wood fillers which are used to fill the pores of open-grain wood. This will be explained later.

Fig. 6-2 Repairing surface defects
with water putty.

If the crack or other defect is deep, the filler should be applied in several applications, allowing each to dry thoroughly before applying the next. The final application should be added so it is slightly above the surface. After drying, it is sanded flush.

Large holes or defects may be plugged. Buttons or plugs are used for round holes. For irregular shapes, a geometric shape (round, square, or triangular) which can be easily duplicated, is cut or chiseled out. A matching piece of the same species of wood is cut and then inserted with glue.

Fig. 6-3 Repairing a large defect. The
plug will replace the mortised section.

Wood buttons are decorative and often used on pine and maple furniture. Chair plugs are also ornamental, but they differ from buttons in that they lack a shoulder and have an oval head. They have slightly tapering sides and will fit snugly when tapped into place. They may be sanded flush and will usually stand out from the wood in which they are used. When matching plugs are desired, plug cutters are used. They can be inserted in a drill press to cut out perfectly round, square-edge plugs. The plugs are installed with glue and should be made to protrude slightly above the surface. When the glue has set, the plugs are sanded smooth and level with the surface.

For small nail holes, the same species of wood is pointed with a pencil sharpener, a little glue is applied, and the wood is driven into the hole. The excess is cut off, and the wood is sanded until level and smooth.

End grain and plywood edge grain to be painted are not difficult to treat. If voids are present, they may simply be filled with wood putty and then sanded. This is followed by applying with a small brush a glue size made by thinning a white glue with water. After allowing the size to dry, unthinned glue is then brushed on. Several coats are given if necessary, sanding lightly between coats. The last coat is scuffed with 6/0 garnet paper, and the necessary undercoats and topcoats of finish material are applied. Properly done, the edges will be as smooth as the top surfaces. If clear finishes are to be used, edge grain of plywood should be trimmed with a suitable wood edging as explained earlier.

SCRAPING

Most lumber used in furniture projects is smoothed and leveled with a jointer or planer before actual construction is begun. Regardless of this, the wood must be given a final smoothing either before or after assembling the component pieces, whichever is easier for the particular project. This final smoothing must precede the finish sanding and is usually done with a cabinet scraper. There are several types and sizes of cabinet scrapers. The cabinet scraper is hand held, and the blade must be scraped or rubbed along the wood surface in the direction of the grain. Each stroke will pick up fine shavings from the surface of the wood. This should be repeated until the surface is glassy smooth.

SANDING

After the defects have been corrected and the surface scraped, the wood must be finish sanded. This is in addition to previous sanding operations. Before sanding, the work must be dusted, preferably with a vacuum cleaner. This is important, as any grit on the surface may cause scratches in the finish. Vacuuming the sander is recommended, also. Sanding should begin with intermediate grit paper, from 2/0 working up to 6/0 for softwood and 7/0 for hardwood. The wood must be sanded with the grain, except for end grain, which must be done crosswise. Care should be used when two grain directions meet. Sanding in a crosswise direction will produce scratches, ripples, and other undesirable blemishes in the final finish.

The degree or fineness of the sanding operation depends on the piece being finished and the type of finish wanted. Sometimes a highly smooth surface is not desirable. Some woods are grain- and figure-free and may be enhanced by introducing controlled scratches. The scratches will fill with stain and darken,

Fig. 6-4 Thorough dusting is
necessary for a superior finish.

thus resulting in an interesting effect. This is an exception however, and most
furniture should be sanded smooth.

Commercial finishers sometimes glue-size the work surface to obtain the
ultimate smoothness. The size acts as a stiffener, causing the surface fibers to
be cut off cleanly by the sanding operation. The home craftsman may achieve
similar results by using water instead of glue. After the final smooth sanding,
the surface is sponged with warm water, allowed to dry overnight, and then
resanded with the same grit paper which was last used.

Fig. 6-5 Sponging the sanded surface
with warm water to raise the surface
fibers.

Care must be exercised when sanding veneers. Too much sanding may go
through the thin veneer layer. If and when shiny spots appear on the sandpaper,
these may be removed by brushing the paper with a fine wire brush or stiff
toothbrush. Shiny spots are caused by loading and will produce scratches on the
wood surface. If the spots persist and remain after brushing, the sandpaper
should be replaced.

When sanding is completed, the surface is dusted carefully, with particular attention given to corners. A vacuum cleaner is used, then a tack rag. Tack rags are sold at most paint supply shops, but one can easily be made by soaking a piece of cheesecloth in thinned varnish, wringing it thoroughly, and then using it with a wiping motion. The sticky cloth will pick up the most minute trace of dust on the work piece.

The finishing procedure described here deals with fine furniture finishing. Painting and antiquing are covered later on.

BLEACHING

The color of wood may be lightened or changed by the application of liquid bleaches, which remove color by oxidation. For example, a mahogany piece may be bleached to remove its red color and then stained to the desired tone. Walnut is a very dark wood, but in industry it is often bleached and then given a medium-tone finish.

Various bleaches are available. Some are single-solution types, such as oxalic acid, a rather weak bleach. Oxalic acid crystals are dissolved in hot water, and the mild solution is applied to the work. If a higher degree of bleaching is desired, a solution of sodium hyposulfite may be applied to the still wet surface. The oxalic acid is mixed at the rate of three ounces of crystals per quart of hot water. The hyposulfite should be mixed in the same proportion.

The two-solution bleaches are very strong and are capable of turning a piece of dark walnut almost white in color. One popular two-solution bleach consists of concentrated hydrogen peroxide and caustic soda. Needless to say, this is a very strong bleach and must be used with great care. Usually the two solutions are premixed just before use in glass or stainless steel containers.

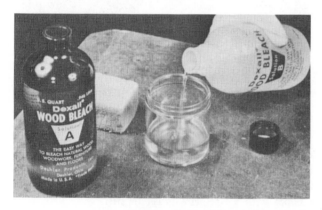

Fig. 6-6 Bleaches are caustic and must be handled with care.

Rubber gloves, face mask, and old clothes should be worn when bleaching wood. The bleach is applied with a cellulose sponge or nylon brush. It is allowed to remain on the work for about a half-hour, then, if necessary, a second application is made.

When the desired degree of bleaching is obtained, the alkaline residue is neutralized with a solution of white vinegar and water, followed by plain water. The work is allowed to dry overnight with ample ventilation. When thoroughly dry, the work should be lightly sanded with 6/0 paper.

Since manufacturers use their own formulations for bleaches, their instructions for the proper use of their products must be followed.

STAINING

After sanding (and bleaching, if necessary), the surface is rubbed down with two or three grades of steel wool to further smooth the surface. All dust and steel wool particles must be removed before stain is applied. The stain enhances the wood by adding color and bringing out the beauty of the grain. Several types of stain are available. The most common are: water stain, oil stain, and NGR stain (non-grain-raising). Stain should be brushed on with a thoroughly clean, good-quality brush.

Water Stains

Consisting of water-soluble aniline dyes and supplied in powder form, water stains must be mixed with boiling water before use. They are very stable and the clearest of all stains, producing sharp and brilliant colors. The colors may be strengthened by adding more powder to the water. The usual mixture is one teaspoonful per quart of water.

Unfortunately, water stains raise the grain of the wood fibers, which means more sanding after the stain has dried. Also, repeated applications may cause failure of glue joints. The stain is applied with a brush or sponge, then wiped with a rag. No matter how it is applied, it will not streak. After overnight drying, it is sanded lightly. To minimize the grain-raising caused by water stains, the surface may be sponged with warm water before the staining operation. The water is allowed to dry, then the surface is sanded lightly.

Fig. 6-7 Sap staining equalizes the color variations of wood.

Water stains are ideally suited for sap staining—the equalizing of color variation between sapwood and heartwood and between different species of wood used in the same furniture piece. Also called shading, sap staining is done before the regular stain is applied. The water stain is applied with a brush to the light areas.

Oil Stains

There are two types of oil stains: pigmented and penetrating. The first type consists of a color pigment mixed in a vehicle, such as linseed oil and turpentine. Although the pigments are opaque, they are thinned to a point where they are almost transparent. In heavier form, the pigments make up the various colored paints. In fact, ordinary paints may be thinned for use as wiping stains). Wiping or pigmented oil stains are easy to use, nongrain-raising, and slow drying.

Pigmented oil stain is applied to a dust-free surface with a brush. The stain should stand a few minutes, then the surface is wiped with the grain with a rag. If the wood varies in color between sapwood and heartwood, a sap stain effect may be obtained by wiping the darker areas first and allowing the stain to remain on the lighter areas a longer time. Overnight drying must be allowed before proceeding with the next step.

Penetrating oil stains consist of dyes dissolved in oil. They color the wood by penetrating the wood fibers. They are completely transparent, easy to apply, and do not streak. Because of their tendency to bleed through sealer coats, penetrating oil stains are not recommended for use under lacquer. Since they do not contain water, penetrating oil stains will not raise the grain of the wood. They are often mixed with fillers to produce a combination stain-filler.

Non-Grain-Raising Stains

Consisting of color dyes mixed with alcohol and glycol, nongrain-raising stains are fast drying and can be recoated within minutes. Because they dry so fast, they are not practical for brush application. However, they are easily applied with a spray gun. These stains are nonbleeding and transparent, and will not fade in sunlight.

WASH COAT

After staining, a wash coat should be applied to the surface to keep the stain from bleeding and to produce a smoother surface for the following filler coat. The wash coat also seals the intermediate area between pores which, to a lesser degree, is also porous. Since fillers have a staining action, the area between pores would unintentionally be given another coat of stain which may not be desirable, especially if the stain is lighter than the filler.

An effective wash coat may be made by mixing one part of four-pound cut white shellac to six to eight parts of alcohol. Too heavy a wash coat will fill the pores and prevent proper filling. The wash coat is applied with a brush and allowed to dry for about one hour before lightly sanding with worn 6/0 paper.

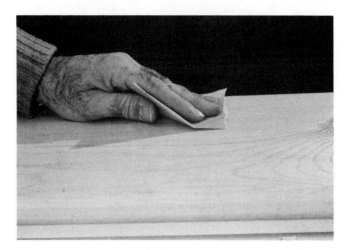

Fig. 6-8 The wash coat of shellac is lightly sanded between coats.

FILLING

The filling process is used on woods with large pores. The material used fills and levels the pores. It also has an effect on the overall color, since the filler used may be lighter, the same as, or darker than the wood tone which is being finished. Fillers are made in liquid and paste forms. The liquid type is generally used on fairly close-grained woods, such as cherry, maple, birch, and gum. Tight-grained woods, such as pine, basswood, and poplar, do not require fillers.

Paste Fillers

Paste fillers are heavy-bodied materials made with silex, which is an inert, colorless, finely ground rock. Paste fillers are mixed with oil and have the consistency of peanut butter. In use, they are thinned with turpentine, naphtha, or benzine to the thickness of heavy cream. They may be purchased in a natural color, which is an off-white, or in various wood tones. The natural may be used as is, or it may be colored using oil stains, depending on the finish desired. Paint tinting universal colors may also be used for coloring the paste fillers.

Paste filler should be applied with a stiff brush, with and across the grain. A small area at a time is worked, while the material in the container is constantly stirred, as it has a tendency to settle. After the filler has flattened or become dull—about fifteen minutes depending on air circulation, temperature, and humidity conditions—it is ready to be "packed in" to the pores. Such coarse

Fig. 6-9 *Paste fillers are tinted with universal colors.*

rags as toweling or burlap work best. The filler is rubbed briskly across the grain and packed into the pores, while the excess filler is removed from the surface. Sticks or small brushes are used to remove filler from corners and carvings.

After the excess filler has been removed, a clean soft cloth is used to wipe the surface lightly across the grain, with a final light wipe with the grain to remove any fingerprints or streaks. This last wipe must be carefully executed so that none of the material in the pores of the wood is removed.

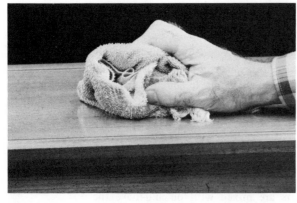

Fig. 6-10 *Paste filler is packed into the pores of open-grained wood.*

Sometimes it is necessary to apply a second coat of filler. This may be determined by examining the filled pores with a powerful magnifier. They should be level, smooth, and without gaps.

The filler must dry overnight. Some fillers may require up to forty-eight hours drying time, so it is best to follow the manufacturers' recommendations.

Liquid Fillers

The same procedure used for paste fillers may be followed for liquid fillers. Liquid fillers may be made by adding sufficient thinner to paste fillers. The thinned material is then applied with a brush.

126

Cloths or rags used to wipe off fillers should not be left piled in a heap, as they may ignite due to spontaneous combustion. After use, they should be spread out to dry or stored under water.

After drying, the filled surface must be sealed to provide a foundation for the topcoats and also to seal in the stain and filler coats. If the topcoat is to be lacquer, a sanding sealer should be used. For a varnish finish, the sealer should be shellac. The sealer should be allowed to dry and then sanded lightly with 6/0 paper, followed by wiping with a tack rag.

GLAZING

Wiping glaze is used for shading and highlighting. It may also be used to correct variations in wood color, especially when two or more species are used in the same piece. Normally, however, color variation is corrected in the staining phase.

Glazing liquids are available ready-made in various colors. For a homemade glaze, Japan colors are mixed with benzine. The glaze is applied to the surface with a brush, rag, or spray. Then, using a soft brush vertically, the surface is wiped, blended, and lightly stroked in the direction of the grain. This is followed by cross-brushing to lay a uniform film over the entire surface. The stroking along the direction of the grain is then repeated, with the brush kept fairly dry during the entire operation by periodically wiping it on a dry, lint-free cloth.

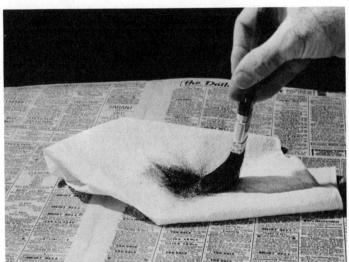

Fig. 6-11 The glazing brush is kept dry by periodically wiping it with a lint-free cloth.

To highlight the center of a panel or tabletop, the glaze must be blended out toward the edges so that little remains in the center. The color is allowed to build up around the edges and corners and around the moldings. The same procedure is used to highlight carvings. Further highlighting may be accomplished with steel wool after the glaze dries.

Following the glazing, a protective topcoat is required.

Fig. 6-12 Highlighting with steel wool.

SPATTERING

Often used to give furniture an antique appearance, spattering consists of a series of dark specks applied in a random pattern over the entire surface. Spattering is usually done after the first topcoat has been put on, but it may be applied at any stage after staining—by itself or combined with distressing marks. The specking is accomplished by flicking a stiff, short-bristled brush which has been lightly dipped into a mixture of lampblack and turpentine. The brush is wiped lightly on newspaper before flicking to remove excess material and held vertically upright. Then the bristles are pulled back and released smartly, with small spots of varying size splattering onto the work. The drier the brush, the smaller the spots. If the results are unsatisfactory, the spots may be wiped clean with mineral spirits and the process repeated.

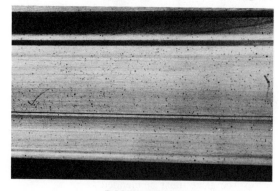

Fig. 6-13 Spatter is applied by flicking a stiff-bristled brush dipped into a solution of lampblack. This piece was done with a toothbrush.

DISTRESSING

Another technique used to give a realistic aged appearance to furniture is called distressing. This technique may be obtained physically by denting the work with such items as chains, coral rock, awls, nail heads, files, knives, etc.,

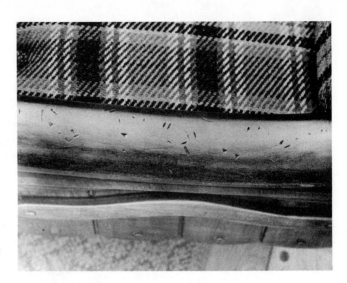

Fig. 6-14 A close-up of distressed furniture.

or anything that will give the appearance of wear and age. These operations are usually done before the finishing operations on the raw wood.

The second type of distressing is executed in conjunction with the specking or afterwards, using a small brush or distressing crayon. Regular crayons may be substituted but, if applied heavily, may cause soft spots in the following topcoats. Small wormlike marks are randomly made on the surface to give the distressed appearance.

TOPCOATS

Various materials may be used as topcoats for final finishing of furniture. The most commonly used are lacquer, varnish, shellac, and synthetics. Actually, most of the above-mentioned materials are synthetics, but in this discussion, the synthetics referred to are the polyesters, polyurethanes, and similar products. A good topcoat should be resistant to water and beverage damage, withstand cracking, and be tough enough to resist scratching and marring. The finishes may impart a high gloss, a semigloss, or be dead flat.

Lacquer

Lacquers may be applied by brush or spray. The brushing type is formulated to dry slowly. The most common types of lacquer used in woodworking are made with nitrocellulose, derived mainly from cotton. Various additions give it the necessary qualities which make it suitable for wood finishing. Its fast-drying feature is one of the reasons it is widely used in the furniture industry, as this speeds up production and also minimizes the dust-settling problem with clear finishes.

Spraying lacquer must be thinned with lacquer thinner. Since there are so many formulations for making lacquer, it is important to use the specific thinner recommended by the manufacturer, as the products must be compatible. The amount of thinning is important and depends on the equipment being used.

*Fig. 6-15 Mixing
lacquer with thinner.*

The problem encountered most often by the novice when spraying is the lack of proper atomization. Unthinned lacquer is of syruplike consistency and, if not thin enough for the equipment, will leave the spray gun as large droplets. Also, too heavy a mixture is apt to cause runs. Three or four coats of lacquer should be applied, sanding lightly between coats. The section on spraying describes the proper technique for applying the finish.

Brushing lacquer is used as it comes from the can. If necessary, it may be thinned with lacquer thinner. Some stains will bleed if the lacquer is brushed on directly without a sealer coat to act as a barrier. To prevent this, a thin coat of shellac is brushed on and allowed to dry thoroughly. Then the surface is lightly sanded and dusted.

The lacquer should be applied with a good soft brush. The brush should be loaded and the material applied quickly without brushing back and forth. Each coat dries for several hours, and the surface is lightly sanded between coats. The sanding is necessary because tiny fibers of wood pull up and become stiffened when the topcoat dries. Just a few light passes with the grain of the wood is all that is required. The final coat should be rubbed as explained at the end of this section.

Varnish

Although it produces a beautiful finish, varnish is difficult to use because of its slow-drying quality. Dust is the enemy of any finish, and since varnish is slow to dry, dust is an ever-present problem. In the past, some varnishes took as long as forty-eight hours to dry; therefore, the work had to be done in special dust-free rooms. Modern varnishes dry in about four to six hours, so there is still plenty of time for dust (and bugs) to settle in it. Varnish is a mixture of resins and thinners and can produce glossy, semiglossy, or flat finishes.

The advantages in using varnish are its ease of application and its high water and alcohol resistance. It has good coverage, and because it dries so slowly, it is self-leveling, thus minimizing brush marks. Care must be exercised when working on vertical surfaces. Too much varnish has a tendency to run and sag. The first varnish coat should be thinned if the work lacks a sealer. Two full coats with light sanding between coats is the usual procedure. During application, room and varnish temperature should be seventy degrees Fahrenheit or warmer.

Although a lint-free cloth may be used, it is preferable to use a good quality bristle brush to apply varnish. The varnish should not be stirred in the can, and the bristles of the brush should not be dragged against the rim of the can, since this may cause air bubbles to form in the varnish. The varnish is applied liberally to the wood surface, brushing first parallel to the grain, then crosswise, then finishing off with a very light stroke parallel to the grain. Each coat of varnish should dry thoroughly, followed by sanding and dusting with a tack rag before the next coat is applied. The final rubbing and polishing will take care of any bubbles or excess gloss in the finish.

Shellac

The resinous secretion of certain insects found in India is dissolved in alcohol to make shellac. Widely used in furniture finishing as a sealer and also as a topcoat, shellac is not recommended for tabletops because it is not waterproof and is affected by alcoholic beverages and strong soaps. Fast-drying and easy to apply, shellac is available in white or orange but may be tinted with aniline dyes. Shellac is usually sold in the liquid form, but most professionals use it in its flake form, mixing the flakes with alcohol as needed, since shellac goes stale in its liquid form. In its liquid form, shellac is sold by the "cut," which signifies its concentration or dilution. A four-pound cut means that four pounds of flakes were dissolved in one gallon of denatured alcohol.

Because shellac does deteriorate with age, reputable manufacturers date their product. The date is usually stamped on the lid of the container. Stale shellac should be avoided, as it will not dry properly and will leave a sticky residue on the surface.

In use, shellac is diluted with denatured alcohol. The amount of thinning depends on its intended use. As a sealer before staining, a four-pound cut should be diluted in the proportion of one to eight, i.e., one part of shellac to eight parts of alcohol. For use as a topcoat, a one-lb. cut is about right. To get this from a four-lb. cut, one part of shellac is mixed to two parts of alcohol. A handy reference table follows here, showing how to dilute stock four- and five-pound cuts of shellac to obtain a desired cut.

Stock "Cut"	"Cut" Desired	Alcohol Volume	Shellac Volume
4 lb.	1 lb.	2 qt.	1 qt.
4 lb.	2 lb.	1-1/2 pt.	1 qt.
4 lb.	3 lb.	1/2 pt.	1 qt.
5 lb.	1 lb.	5-1/3 pt.	1 qt.
5 lb.	2 lb.	1 qt.	1 qt.
5 lb.	3 lb.	14 fl. oz.	1 qt.

When applying shellac, it should be noted that several thin coats are better than one heavy coat. When thinned, it is easier to apply and dries faster. Under normal weather conditions, recoating may be done in about one hour; in humid weather, the drying period is longer.

The shellac is applied freely with a fully loaded brush, first across then with the grain, with each stroke being lapped slightly. Brush marks will level as the shellac dries. A piece of 3/0 steel wool is rubbed between each coat. The surface is then dusted, and subsequent coats are applied in the same manner. Three coats should be sufficient. For a satin finish, the final coat is rubbed with 3/0 steel wool, and a coat of paste wax serves as the finish. For a not-so-dull finish, the surface should be rubbed with a finer steel wool—such as 5/0 or 6/0—and then wax applied.

Polyurethanes

Although similar to varnish, polyurethanes dry more quickly and thus minimize the dust problem. They are tough, water and heat resistant, and are used like varnish, except that sanding between coats is not necessary unless too much time has elapsed before reapplication. Manufacturers' instructions specify the time limits for recoating. Humidity has no detrimental effect on the application of these products. Actually, high humidity hastens the hardening of the polyurethanes.

When recoated within the prescribed times, the coats are able to fuse chemically; otherwise, scuffing with 220-grit paper is needed to provide a "bite" for the following coats. The material is applied unthinned with a brush or roller. Thinning is necessary for spraying. Polyurethanes are made in gloss and satin finish. The gloss material dries with a very high luster which can be toned down with 4/0 steel wool.

Linseed Oil

Although this process gives wood a natural mellow luster which is very attractive, linseed oil applications are time-consuming. The finish is resistant to heat and scratches, but is not water resistant. Commercially purchased boiled linseed oil (a product of flaxseed) is thinned with turpentine, spread liberally over the wood surface with a thick pad of cloth, and allowed to soak in for about an hour. The surface is then rubbed briskly with the same oily pad, excess oil is wiped off with clean cloths, and the work is allowed to dry overnight. When thoroughly dry, the oiling process is repeated. (In damp weather it may take a week or longer to dry between coats). At least three applications are necessary to produce a durable, attractive finish. The more often the process is repeated, the better the finish. This should be repeated once or twice a year, as the oil has a tendency to dry out. Used cloths should be stored under water or spread out flat to dry, as they are highly combustible.

Rubbing and Polishing

A professional appearance is added to furniture by rubbing and polishing. This should be done only after the topcoats are thoroughly dry. Sprayed lacquer may be rubbed in several hours, brushed lacquer should dry overnight, and varnish should dry in about a week.

Rubbing is done with fine abrasives and a lubricant to produce a level, smooth surface and to remove any irregularities that may show up in the final topcoat. It may be done with very fine abrasive paper, steel wool, pumice, and other abrasives. The type of abrasive used depends on the material selected for the topcoat and on the desired results. The objective in rubbing is to cut the surface to eliminate low spots, dust, and pebbling or "orange peel." In the past, abrasive powders were used exclusively, but the trend now is to use special sandpaper made for this purpose.

Some finishers start with lubricated sandpaper, followed by rubbing compound. If the topcoat is in poor condition, the rubbing should be started with coarser grits, progressively working down to the finest. For example, one should start with 360-grit and finish with 400-grit wet-dry paper. (Note: 360-grit paper is not coarse, except when compared to 400-grit paper). The paper is supported with a felt pad and used wet with water or rubbing oil. The lubricant keeps the paper from loading up. Linseed oil soap and water makes an ideal lubricant. As the rubbing progresses with the finer papers, the scratches diminish and the sheen increases. The cutting action of the abrasive paper must be carefully observed, however, as excessive rubbing may cut through the finish.

The 400-grit paper will produce a good satin finish, but for increased smoothness, a 500-grit paper is recommended. For an even smoother finish, rubbing compound may be used after the sanding. The compound also reaches into the low spots in the finish. For varnish, the abrasive powder should be pumice and water. (Pumice is a fine powder derived from volcanoes.) Lacquer finishes are harder and require tougher abrasives. When made into a paste, these compounds are graded coarse and fine. The coarse is used to speed up the cutting action; the finer grade is used for the final rubbing to produce a highly smooth surface. The rubbing compound is applied with a water-dampened cloth, and, if thinning of the paste is required, water or naphtha may be used. The coarse compound will leave a smooth but satin finish. The fine compound will yield a mirrorlike finish. After rubbing is completed, the surface should be cleaned thoroughly with naphtha to remove all rubbing sludge and allowed to dry completely. Then it is polished with 4/0 steel wool, and a paste or liquid furniture wax is applied.

Painting

Paints for interior use are made in flat, semigloss, and gloss finishes. For furniture, the gloss and semigloss types are generally used. As a rule, the gloss enamels are the most durable. Enamels are available in three types: alkyd-base, latex-base, and polyurethane-base. The alkyd and polyurethane types require a solvent-type thinner. The latex type uses water as a solvent. Colored lacquer is also used for wood and, like clear lacquer, requires lacquer thinner as a solvent and is fast-drying.

Before painting, furniture must be sanded smooth, and all nail holes and voids filled. For absorbent edge grain, as found in plywood, the edges are glue-sized with thinned white glue, sanded when dry, and a second coat applied if necessary. Following the filling and sanding, an appropriate undercoater, recommended by the paint manufacturer, is applied. The undercoater provides a good smooth base for the enamel or lacquer. For better coverage of the top-coat, the undercoater may be tinted.

Topcoats are brushed or sprayed on after the undercoat has thoroughly dried. The first coat may be thinned slightly for easier application. The second coat is applied straight, without thinning. Ample drying time between coats is allowed and the surface is scuffed with 6/0 paper to give the surface tooth. Two coats of enamel brushed on are usually sufficient. Too many coats of enamel may cause such problems as chipping.

Sprayed colored lacquer usually requires three coats, because the material is applied much thinner than the enamels. The same procedure is followed as for enameling, with the intermediate coats being sanded and dusted before additional coats are added. Normally the last coat is not sanded or rubbed, although it may be for a low-luster, smooth finish.

Lacquer spraying is ideal for two-tone work. Masking tape and newspaper may be used to protect areas which have previously been painted or decorated.

Fig. 6-16 Masking tape and newspaper are used to control areas to be sprayed.

Enamels and lacquers are available in aerosol cans. They are suitable for small jobs and for touching up, but they are not recommended for large pieces as they are too expensive and lack body, and it is difficult to obtain even coverage over a large area.

Antiquing

A method of finishing in which a piece is made to look old or antique by the application of paints and glazes is known as antiquing. Physical distressing is also used to simulate age. The method works equally well on old and new furniture. In the first method, a base coat of opaque enamel is applied to the bare or previously finished wood. This base coat may be in bright colors or in subdued wood tones. Contrasting glaze colors are applied to the dried base coat, then wiped with cloth, brush, sponge, or other items to achieve various effects. Dents and scratches are not normally objectionable in this type of finish; however, since the base coat is opaque, the defects may easily be eliminated if desired.

If the piece to be antiqued is old, all exposed hardware, such as hinges, knobs, and pulls should be removed. The surface is washed to remove all traces of polishes and waxes. This is done with a solution of ammonia and water, but care must be taken not to slosh the water on too generously, as the glue joints may be weakened. A wrung-out cloth or sponge is usually sufficient.

All loose joints must be glued, and, if defects are to be filled, a suitable wood putty or spackle may be used. After allowing the surface to dry, it may be sanded lightly. If the filled area is large, the sanding may produce a different texture between the patched area and the surrounding surface. In such cases, sanding the entire surface is recommended.

Sanding is also indicated on cracking or peeling surfaces. If not correctable by sanding, it may be necessary to remove the old finish entirely. This is covered in the section on refinishing.

If physical distressing is desired, it is done after the surface has been cleaned and repaired, or on new work after the piece has been completed and before the final sanding. Distressing may be accomplished with any number of handy objects: chains, ice pick, hammer, knife, coral rock, rasp, buckshot, etc.

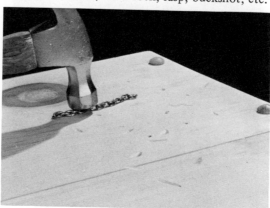

Fig. 6-17 A chain is one of the many items that may be used for distressing.

The purpose of distressing is to "work" the piece over to give it wear marks and blemishes, such as it would get in normal usage over the years. Although anything goes in this process, the tendency is to overdo it. Perhaps the best way to judge the amount of distressing is to study genuine antiques and try to imitate them. Care should be taken not to sever the wood fibers when adding blemishes. The surface should be dented but not broken, except for worm holes and similar marks which are made with sharp, pointed objects. Worn edges are best made with files, spokeshaves, or rough sandpaper. Corners are rounded and edges are given an unevenness with any of these tools. Flat surfaces may also be dished or hollowed out using a disc sander.

After distressing is completed, the abrasions are sanded lightly to remove any sharp abrasion marks. If the surface to be finished has a smooth or glossy surface, it should be sanded to provide tooth for the base coat. Liquid sanding preparations are available for this purpose. If one of these is used, the manufacturer's directions must be followed, with particular attention paid to drying time. The base coat is applied with brush or spray. If more than one coat of base is required, sanding should be done between the coats. One coat is usually sufficient on old work, but two are recommended for raw wood. If a brush is employed, it should be used with the grain.

After the base coat has dried (alkyds take longer than latex), the glaze may be applied. Some workers prefer to give the base coat a thin application of quick-drying sealer. This permits easy removal of the glaze if the results are not satisfactory. The process is then repeated.

The glaze is applied liberally with a brush, working it into every crack and corner. Grain direction is not important at this stage. The entire piece should not be glazed at one time; instead, one surface at a time should be covered.

The glaze should stand until it starts to dull, then the excess glaze is wiped with a soft cloth or facial tissues, working from the center out toward the edges. If too much material has been wiped away, more should be brushed on, allowing time for it to dull, and then the process repeated. Now the paper

Fig. 6-18 Filling nail heads with spackle.

or cloth is replaced with a soft, dry brush and light strokes are taken with the grain. The material is allowed to build up near the edges and at the corners. The brush is kept dry by wiping it on newspapers, and long, light strokes are continually taken with the grain of the wood. When done properly, the brush marks will not show; only a gradual darkening of the glaze from highlight to shading will result.

Some glazes are made with a sealing agent and require no further treatment. Otherwise, the glazed surface should be sealed after it is completely dry. Most glaze manufacturers recommend a suitable sealer for their product. The surface must be dry, or damage to the glazed finish may result. Before the sealer is applied, additional highlighting may be accomplished by the use of fine steel wool. Patience is required for this operation. Very light sweeping strokes are made so that the removal of glaze is subtle, without abrupt changes in the tone.

Fig. 6-19 Final sanding operation before applying finish.

Fig. 6-20 A tack rag picks up all traces of dust.

Fig. 6-21 Applying a latex base coat.

Fig. 6-22 Glaze is applied after the base coat has dried.

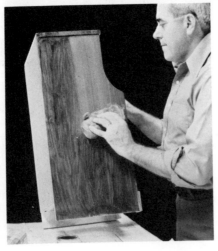

Fig. 6-23 Wiping excess glaze with a soft cloth.

REFINISHING

Old finishes may be removed mechanically by sanding or scraping, but usually it is easier to use chemical removers. These soften the finish, which is then wiped or, in some cases, scraped off. Removers are either liquid, cream, or pastelike in consistency. Most contain wax retarders, which slow down evaporation, allowing the chemical time to soften the paint. In some removers the wax must be washed out of the wood. In others, the wax residue does not remain on the wood. The latter removers are usually more expensive than the cleanup type.

Removers will remove most paints and varnishes, but few, if any, will remove some latex paints. If one is confronted with this problem, lacquer thinner should be tried. It is not sold for this purpose, but it works. Because it evaporates so fast, paper towels may have to be saturated and covered with aluminum foil, which will keep the thinner on the paint long enough to soften it.

Most chemical removers are flammable, and all give off toxic fumes which should be avoided even for short periods of time. If possible, it is best to work outdoors where flames and fumes will not be a problem.

The work area should be well protected with newspapers, and protective clothing, gloves, and face mask or goggles should be worn. The remover is then brushed on the piece and allowed to stand. When the finish has softened, it is removed by scraper or washed off with water, depending on the product used.

After the old finish has been removed and the piece has dried, a light sanding is recommended, especially if the piece is to be given a stain finish. The sanding will ensure that the stain will take evenly.

SPRAY PAINTING AND FINISHING

At one time, spray painting and finishing was considered a craft for the professional only, but this is no longer true. Spraying equipment is found in many home workshops nowadays, alongside other power and hand tools.

Fig. 6-24 Modern spray equipment is easy to use.

Spray painting has become very popular, due, no doubt, to its relatively low cost and the easy availability of quality spray products. With such equipment at his disposal, the woodworker may obtain excellent results with the least amount of time and effort. The spraying referred to here is not to be confused with aerosol can spraying. The latter is fine for touch-up work and for very small items but not suitable for furniture finishing and refinishing.

Basically, spraying equipment consists of a compressor and spray gun. The compressor produces air at higher than atmospheric pressure. The air passes through the gun where it atomizes the finishing material into a fine mist. The air pressure from the gun also aids in depositing the fine particles onto the work surface.

There are two popular types of compressors widely used today: the diaphragm type and the piston type. The diaphragm compressor utilizes a rubberized cloth diaphragm which acts as piston. On the intake stroke, free air is pulled into a chamber through a one-way valve. On the compression stroke, the air is compressed and forced out under pressure. High pressures are not possible with this type of compressor.

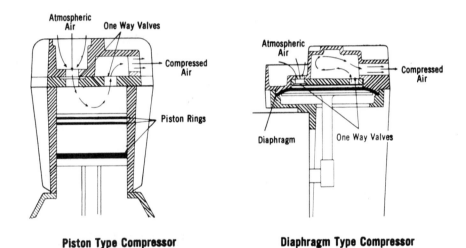

Piston Type Compressor   **Diaphragm Type Compressor**

Fig. 6–25 Two types of compressors.

The piston-type compressor works much like a gasoline engine. Air is drawn into the chamber on the downstroke of the piston. A one-way valve prevents the air from escaping through the same port. On the upstroke of the piston, the air is compressed and forced out of the exhaust port under pressure. High pressures and greater volumes of air are obtainable with this type of compressor.

Air from a diaphragm-type compressor has a pulsating quality. In the piston-type system, the compressed air is stored in a tank, thus providing a steady source of air. A regulator on the tank maintains constant and correct air pressure at the gun.

Fig. 6-26 The compressor must be of sufficient capacity to supply a steady source of air to the gun.

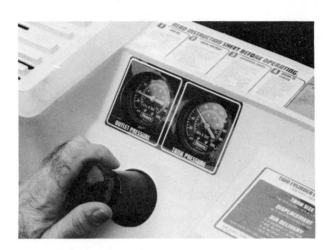

Fig. 6-27 The regulator is set to deliver the required pressure at the gun.

Compressors are rated by the volume of air they can produce and by the pressure delivered at the spray nozzle. The volume of air is measured in cubic feet of air per minute (CFM), and the pressure as pounds per square inch (PSI). The higher the CFM, the faster the spraying process; the higher the PSI, the heavier the finishing material that can be sprayed.

Spray guns are of three types: bleeder, pressure-feed and siphon-feed. The bleeder-type gun is used mostly with continuously running compressors. The trigger controls only the finish material as air is constantly "bleeding" through the nozzle. In the nonbleeder type, air is released only when the trigger is pulled. This allows the operator to control both finish material and air. Non-bleeder guns are used only with tank-type compressors. Pressure-feed guns are mounted to air-tight containers. Air pressure on the liquid to be sprayed forces it up to the gun nozzle where it is atomized and deposited on the work. This type is ideal for heavy-bodied finishes. Siphon-feed guns create a partial vacuum in the material container (gun cup), thus drawing the liquid into the air stream where it is atomized at the nozzle.

141

The gun nozzle may be of internal or external mix design. In the internal mix, nozzle fluid and air combine within the nozzle thus making them better suited for heavy, slow-drying materials, such as enamels and polyurethanes. The external mix nozzle combines air and fluid outside the nozzle and is ideally suited for fast-drying thinner materials. In both types, the action of air and the nozzle tip cause the material to be atomized. The air traveling at high speed carries the finely divided material to the work surface.

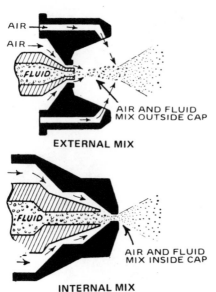

Fig. 6-28 Two types of spray gun nozzles.

A spray booth is ideal for spraying as over-spray and fumes are expelled from the room safely. However, spray booths require special exhaust systems, and this could be a problem for most home craftsmen. It is far easier to simply spray outdoors on a driveway or back yard. Dust is not a problem when using lacquers, as they dry fast, unlike varnishes and enamels. Spraying should never be done indoors without a proper exhaust system. Not only are the fumes toxic, but most are highly explosive as well. Nose and mouth should be covered with a mask to prevent inhalation of spray, and a cap worn on the head to keep the hair clean.

Good spraying requires lots of practice, and cardboard boxes are ideal for this purpose. They may be used to adjust the spray pattern and to practice applying the material.

Proper control of the spray gun is essential to ensure a smooth, even finish. If the spray gun is held too close to the work, the material will sag or run. If held too far away from the work, the material reaches the surface in a partially dry state, resulting in a sandy finish. There is no set rule, but keeping the nozzle about six or eight inches from the work should suffice. Two common faults encountered by the beginner are improper motion and hesitation. The gun must be moved parallel to the work. This is done by moving the arm in a straight line thus ensuring an equal deposit of material. Arcing results when only the wrist is moved and the material is deposited unevenly. The gun should be kept ninety degrees to the work surface at all times.

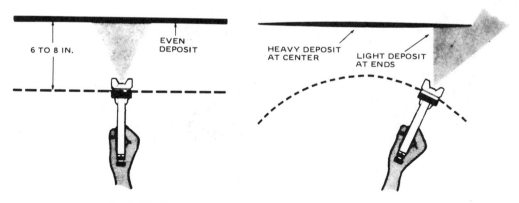

Fig. 6-29 Correct and incorrect stroking procedures.

If the gun is stopped momentarily, too much material will be deposited in one spot, causing runs or sags. This will also happen if the material being sprayed is too thin.

The starting stroke should begin off the work, and the trigger pulled just as it approaches the work. The trigger is released just before the end of the stroke. The ideal pattern is evenly shaped, either round or oval. The oval pattern (fan-shaped) is usually used for wide surfaces. The pattern is changed from vertical to horizontal by rotating the spray gun nozzle ninety degrees. The amount of material leaving the nozzle is controlled by adjusting the fluid control knob.

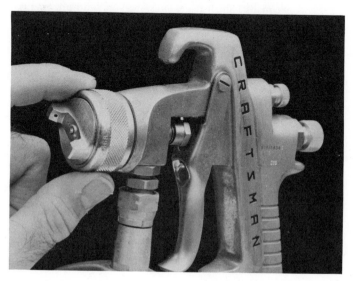

Fig. 6-30 Rotating the nozzle changes the spray pattern.

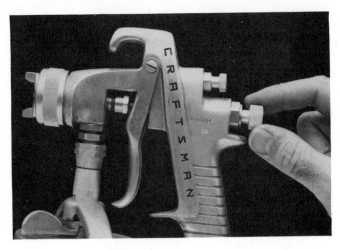

Fig. 6-31 Air and fluid controls
are at the rear of the gun.

Each stroke is overlapped about fifty percent to ensure a uniform film deposit over the entire surface. As a guide, the center of the nozzle may be aimed at the edge of the last stroke.

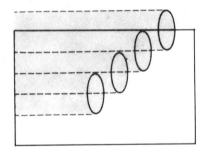

Fig. 6-32 Overlapping strokes 50 percent
ensures complete coverage.

Corners are sprayed by holding the gun so both surfaces are sprayed equally. Small panels may be sprayed horizontally or vertically, but long panels should be sprayed in the short direction.

Fig. 6-33 The corners inside and out are sprayed diagonally.

144

There is one exception to the rule requiring that the gun be moved in a straight line: when the work surface is curved, the gun should move in the same arc as the work.

When spraying such a piece as a table, the edges should be sprayed first, then the top. The actual sequence in spraying a table follows. The inside areas of the legs are sprayed first, then the outsides, then the table edges, and finally the top surface. When spraying a flat surface at an angle, it should always be sprayed from the near side, to allow the overspray to fall on the uncoated area.

Stain may be applied to furniture far more efficiently by spraying than by brushing. However, care must be taken not to overspray.

Fig. 6-34 Applying stain with a sprayer is fast and efficient.

Chapter 7

SIMPLE FURNITURE PROJECTS

Having reviewed the basics of building furniture, it is now time to test the builder's skill. The majority of the pieces shown in this chapter have been designed with simplicity in mind as an encouragement for the novice woodworker. All of the pieces may be made with ordinary hand and power tools. At first glance, some of them may appear difficult to construct, but a careful study of the drawings will show that the pieces are not very complicated.

All of the furniture pieces shown in this chapter are of original design. They are attractive, functional, and easy to fabricate. Building furniture is a rewarding hobby or craft; a good woodworker will derive as much satisfaction and pride from the actual building of the piece as he will later in using and displaying it.

Most of the materials and hardware are readily available at local lumberyards and hardware stores. Some specialty items may be difficult to obtain in outlying areas, and nothing is more frustrating than not being able to find a source of supply. To avoid such disappointment, at the end of this chapter is a source list for some of the items used in these projects that are difficult to obtain.

Drawer construction has intentionally been kept simple. Each drawer is made with a double front, which is an excellent way to make a good, sturdy drawer fast. For the woodworker with more experience, perhaps drawers with more complex construction may be desirable. The drawers shown here are made with rabbets and dadoes. However, they could also be made with dovetails, lock joints, milled-shaper joints, and many others. Should this type of construction be used, the overall sizes of the drawers should be kept the same, but the component sizes may be changed as necessary.

The various projects containing drawers list the sizes and quantities of the necessary parts. For construction details, the drawings shown in this chapter

147

may be consulted. Because it differs slightly, the drawer details for the bed are shown on the page with the drawing for the bed construction.

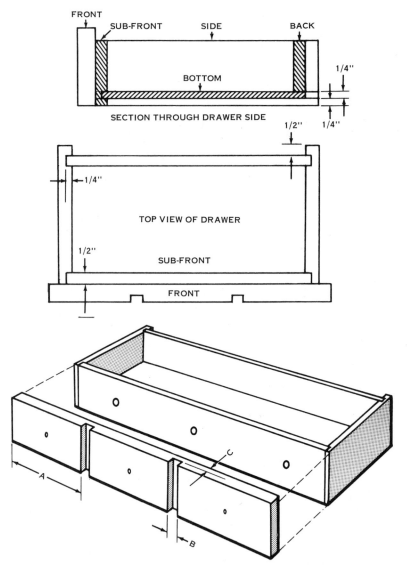

Fig. 7-1 *Details for drawers shown in the various projects. The dadoes are used only in those drawers with multiple fronts.*

To give the effect of multiple drawers, the front panel of a drawer may be divided into equal parts and then dadoed. This is especially useful when many small drawers are involved. The result is one large drawer that looks from the outside like two, three, or even more drawers. (See the sugar bin end table project as an example.) If the drawer edges are to be rounded, as they often are in early American pieces, this may be done by hand or with a router.

The procedure is as follows: The dado is cut in the usual manner with a router. The edges of the dado are then rounded by replacing the cutter with a two-piece rounding bit from which the pilot has been removed. The router is guided by clamping a straightedge parallel to the dado. The spacing of the straightedge depends on the size of the router base. One edge is shaped, then the straightedge is moved to the opposite side and the process repeated.

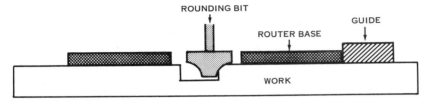

Fig. 7-2 Method of rounding the dado between drawer fronts.

When installing the front panel of double-front drawers, two screw holes are bored through the subfront, with the holes made about 3/32 of an inch larger than the screw shank. Then the front is mounted by driving two round-head screws from inside the drawer. Glue should not be used. The drawer is then checked for fit; if necessary, the screws are loosened slightly, and the front is shifted as needed to center it over the opening. A few brads are driven from inside the drawer through the subfront and part way into the front. Then the screws are removed, and the front is pulled away from the subfront, leaving the brads protruding from the surface. Then glue is applied, the brads are realigned, and the pieces are joined permanently.

If the front panel of a flush drawer is made a trifle wider than the subfront, the ends may be beveled slightly to prevent the drawer from jamming at the edges when closing. This is especially important when drawers are made without guides.

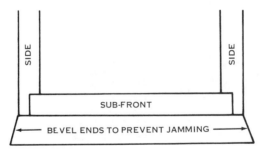

Fig. 7-3 Ends of flush drawer front are beveled to prevent jamming of drawer against cabinet sides.

The drawers in the early American chest utilize commercial guides. These are furnished with installation instructions, which should be consulted before constructing the drawers, as clearance allowances may vary among different manufacturers.

The bottom edge of drawer sides are often waxed to make the drawers operate smoothly. Drawer tacks may also be used for this purpose. A pair of tacks is placed at the rear bottom of the drawer sides. Another pair is used at the front end of the cabinet, positioned so the drawer sides ride over them. Pressure-

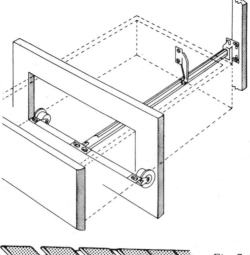

Fig. 7-4 Typical center slide drawer hardware. The mounting bracket fastens to a vertical piece of wood mounted at the rear of the cabinet.

Fig. 7-5 Pressure-sensitive type drawer slides. Mounted to a backing strip, they are peeled off and pressed into place on the drawer and frame.

sensitive slides for drawers are also available. Made of low-friction plastics, the slides are used instead of the tacks.

Some of the furniture projects, such as the chair and the hassock/bench, have padded cushions. These are fairly easy to make using urethane foam and upholstery vinyl with a fabric backing. The problem faced by most novices is how to pull the material tight over the foam pad. This is easily done by using a deep-throat clamp to squeeze the foam while the fabric is being stapled.

The cushion base is usually made of three-eighths-inch or half-inch plywood. A piece of fabric of sufficient size is placed on a flat work surface. On top of this are placed a piece of foam and a piece of plywood, both cut to the size and shape of the cushion. The combination is then squeezed with a clamp until the

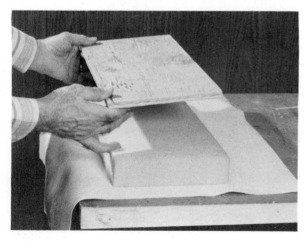

Fig. 7-6 Foam is sandwiched between the fabric and cushion base.

foam is almost flat. Some of the foam which squeezes out may be left, but if the squeeze-out is excessive, it should be trimmed with a sharp knife. The fabric is then draped over the edges and stapled securely to the plywood base. The excess fabric is trimmed, and the clamps removed. The foam will expand when the clamping pressure is released and will form a nicely rounded, wrinkle-free cushion. If deep-throat clamps are not available, a piece of hardwood may be used across the cushion, clamping it at the ends.

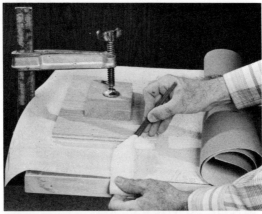

Fig. 7-7 A clamp is used to squeeze the foam almost flat.

Fig. 7-8 Material is wrapped around the edges and stapled.

Fig. 7-9 An alternate method of squeezing the sandwich without using deep-throat clamps.

Fig. 7-10

RUSTIC PICTURE FRAME

This sturdy picture frame with its hand-hewn boards will make a fine addition to a den or dining room. This one is made to fit a twenty-four by thirty-six-inch painting, but the dimensions may be changed to fit any size canvas.

The frame is made in two sections. Since the inside dimensions of the front section are smaller than the rear section, when both are assembled a rabbet is formed to hold the picture. Dowels are used to assemble the front section with two dowels at each joint.

The rugged, worn look may be done before or after the parts are assembled, but it is easier to perform this step before assembly. The hewing may be done with a spokeshave, rasp, rough sandpaper, or a belt sander. The drum part of the sander is used to "gouge" out the indents. The dips should be similar but not identical.

The rear section is somewhat different from the front. The ends are made of separate pieces which are fastened to the end support with three-quarter-inch nails. Before the rear section is assembled, the screw shank holes should be bored, large enough to allow for movement, especially of the small end pieces. When both sections are completed, they are joined with screws by centering the front over the rear. Glue should not be used.

Most oil paintings are mounted on a three-quarter-inch frame which will fit flush into the rabbet. To hold the painting in place, a narrow strip of quarter-inch plywood is fastened along the upper and lower edge of the rear of the frame, allowing it to overhang the back of the picture slightly. Using screws facilitates removal of the painting for cleaning.

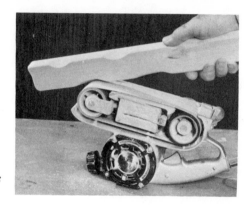

Fig. 7-11 Gouging the frame edges with a belt sander.

Materials List for Picture Frame

Part	Description	Size and Material	Quantity
1	Horizontal rear	3/4 × 5-1/2 × 48 pine	2
2	End rear	3/4 × 5-3/4 × 6 pine	8
3	End support	1/4 × 3-3/4 × 34 plywood	2
4	Vertical front	3/4 × 2-1/4 × 29-1/4 pine	2
5	Horizontal front	3/4 × 2-1/4 × 34-3/4 pine	2
A	Dowel	3/8 × 2	8
B	Screw	1-1/4 – 8 FH	18

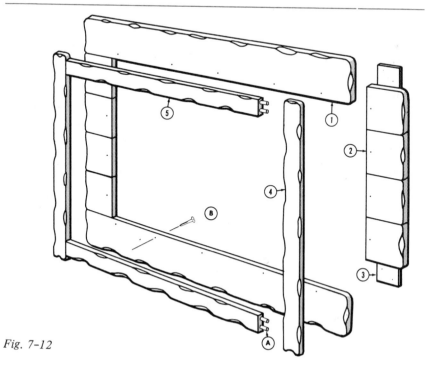

Fig. 7-12

Fig. 7–13

TOTE STOOL

A simple stool that fits easily into any nook or cranny is very handy to have around the house. This version is early American in style and has a hand grip for ease in toting.

The lumber used for this project is 1-1/4-inch and 1-3/4-inch pine, except for the backrest support block, which is 1-1/8-inch stock. The legs were turned on a lathe but, with patience, may be shaped by hand. The backrest and seat are cut with a saber saw. When cutting the circular part of the seat, the blade is tilted fifteen degrees to form the bevel. When cutting the notch for the backrest, the blade is returned to ninety degrees. The holes for the legs are drilled on a 9-3/4-inch diameter hole circle. The holes should be angled toward the center of the seat, using a T-bevel as a guide to align the drill. If a drill press with a tilting table is available, the table is simply tilted eight degrees. A router is used to soften the edges of the seat and back. A 3/8-inch rounding cutter was used for this tote stool.

Materials List for Tote Stool

Part	Description	Size and Material	Quantity
1	Back rest	1-1/4 × 4-1/4 × 23-3/4 pine	1
2	Support block	1-1/8 × 2 × 3-3/8 pine	1
3	Seat	1-3/4 × 13 pine	1
4	Leg	1-3/4 × 15-3/8 pine	4
A	Screw	2-1/4 – 10 FH	6

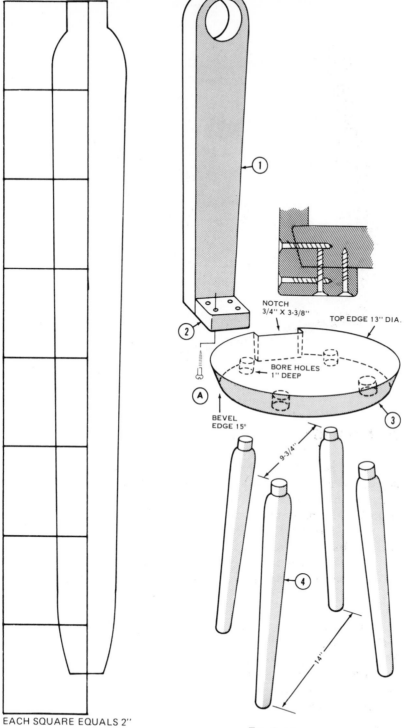

EACH SQUARE EQUALS 2"

NOTCH
3/4" X 3-3/8"

TOP EDGE 13" DIA.

BORE HOLES
1" DEEP

BEVEL
EDGE 15°

9-3/4"

14"

Fig. 7-14

Fig. 7–15

TIERED MAGAZINE RACK

When placed near a favorite chair, this magazine rack is very useful. The stepped compartments hold the magazines so the titles show clearly. The rack is made of half-inch and three-quarter-inch pine boards, and construction is not difficult. The compartment fronts are made to float in blind grooves cut in the side pieces. Screws are used only at the bottom shelf and the top rail. Brads fasten the back panel to the sides and shelf bottoms.

First, the pieces are laid out and cut to size. Then the grooves and rabbets are cut as indicated. The top rail has tenons at each end, and the lower rear edge is rabbeted to receive the back panel. Before assembling, all exposed edges should be rounded.

During assembly, the shelves are centered over the front panel and fastened with 1-1/2-inch finishing nails, which are sunk in the bottom panel and filled in. If desired, screws and plugs may be used here instead.

When the back panel is bradded to the various shelves, the spaces between the shelves are blocked temporarily with scraps of wood to provide a solid surface for nailing. If the surface is not firm, it will be impossible to drive the brads.

Materials List for Tiered Magazine Rack

Part	Description	Size and Material	Quantity
1	End	3/4 × 8-1/2 × 23-7/8 pine	2
2	Top panel	1/2 × 8-3/4 × 20-7/8 pine	1
3	Center panel	1/2 × 9-7/8 × 20-7/8 pine	1
4	Bottom panel	1/2 × 7-3/8 × 20-7/8 pine	1
5	Back panel	1/2 × 5-5/32 × 18-1/2 pine	4
6	Top shelf	3/4 × 2 × 20-3/8 pine	1
7	Center shelf	3/4 × 4-1/2 × 20-3/8 pine	1
8	Bottom shelf	3/4 × 7 × 20-3/8 pine	1
9	Top rail	3/4 × 4-5/8 × 20-5/8 pine	1
A	Screw	1-1/2 – 8 FH – 5/8″ button	6
B	Finishing nail	1-1/2″	12
C	Brads	5/8″	8

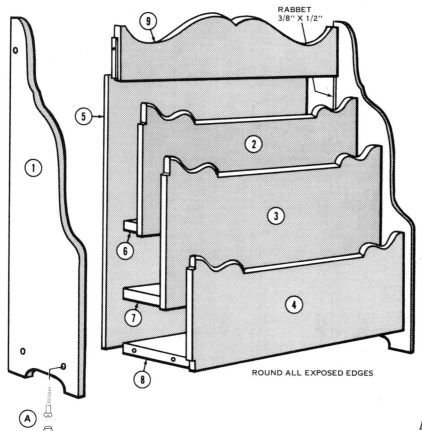

RABBET
3/8″ X 1/2″

ROUND ALL EXPOSED EDGES

Fig. 7-16

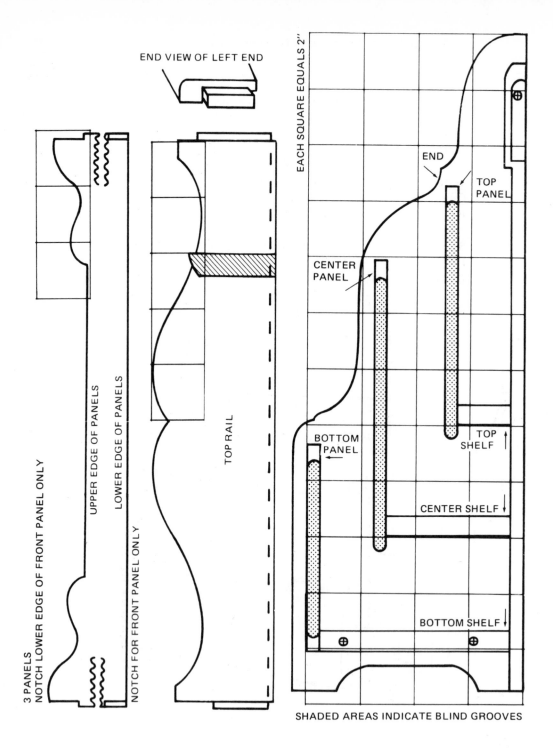

END VIEW OF LEFT END

3 PANELS
NOTCH LOWER EDGE OF FRONT PANEL ONLY

UPPER EDGE OF PANELS

LOWER EDGE OF PANELS

NOTCH FOR FRONT PANEL ONLY

TOP RAIL

EACH SQUARE EQUALS 2"

END

TOP PANEL

CENTER PANEL

BOTTOM PANEL

TOP SHELF

CENTER SHELF

BOTTOM SHELF

SHADED AREAS INDICATE BLIND GROOVES

Fig. 7-17

BOOK RACK

Made of black walnut and contrasting brass rods, this handsome book rack will hold books on display on any desk, table, or counter top. It is elegant in style, yet practical. Except for the four corner posts which are turned on the lathe, the project is rather easy. For those without a lathe, the turnings may be substituted with three-quarter-inch wood dowels or ready-made spindles, which are available at many lumberyards and home-improvement centers. If ready-made spindles are chosen, they should be obtained before starting the project, and the measurements altered as necessary. The spindles may be modified by cutting them to size and whittling new tenons.

First, a layout of the base piece is made on a piece of rigid stock, such as a file folder. It is then cut to shape, taped to the work piece, and the outline is traced. The hole centers are pierced with an awl, the outline is sawed, and all holes are drilled to a quarter-inch uniform depth. If a drill press is used, a backstop is clamped to the table to keep the holes in a straight line.

The rail piece is made by mitering a strip of three-quarter-inch stock after the edges have been shaped with a router. A blind spline cut crossgrain from the same stock strengthens the miter. The spline is placed at the bottom of the rail, and a chisel or router is used to mortise the rail for the spline.

When the rail has been glued, the template made for the base is used to locate the holes. The template is placed upside down on the piece to ensure perfect alignment of the holes.

If the posts are turned on the lathe, they should be sanded, filled, stained, and finished while still in the lathe. The brass rods (or tubes) are cut to length and the ends chamfered slightly to avoid damaging the wood during assembly.

Materials List for Book Rack

Part	Description	Size and Material	Quantity
1	Base	3/4 × 7-7/8 × 16-5/8 walnut	1
2	Post	3/4 × 8 walnut	4
3	Rail end	3/4 × 1 × 7-1/4 walnut	2
4	Rail rear	3/4 × 1 × 15-3/4 walnut	1
5	Brass rod or tubing	5/16 × 8 brass	19
6	Spline	1/8 × 1/2 × 1 walnut	2

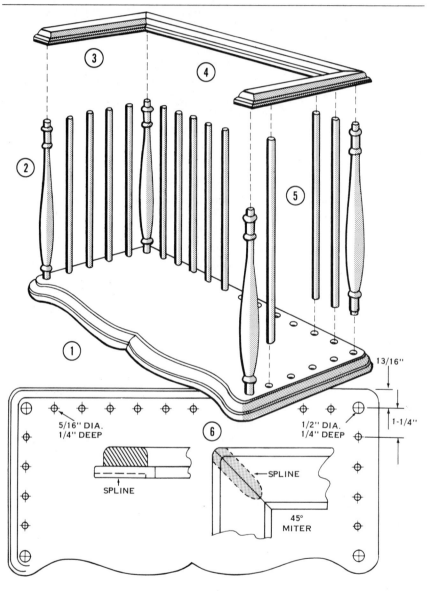

Fig. 7-18

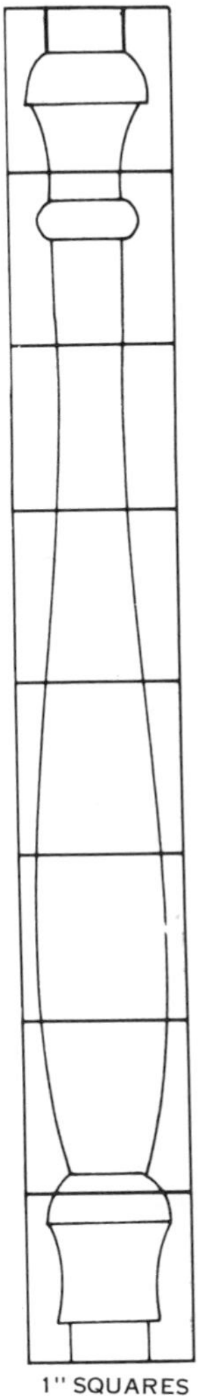

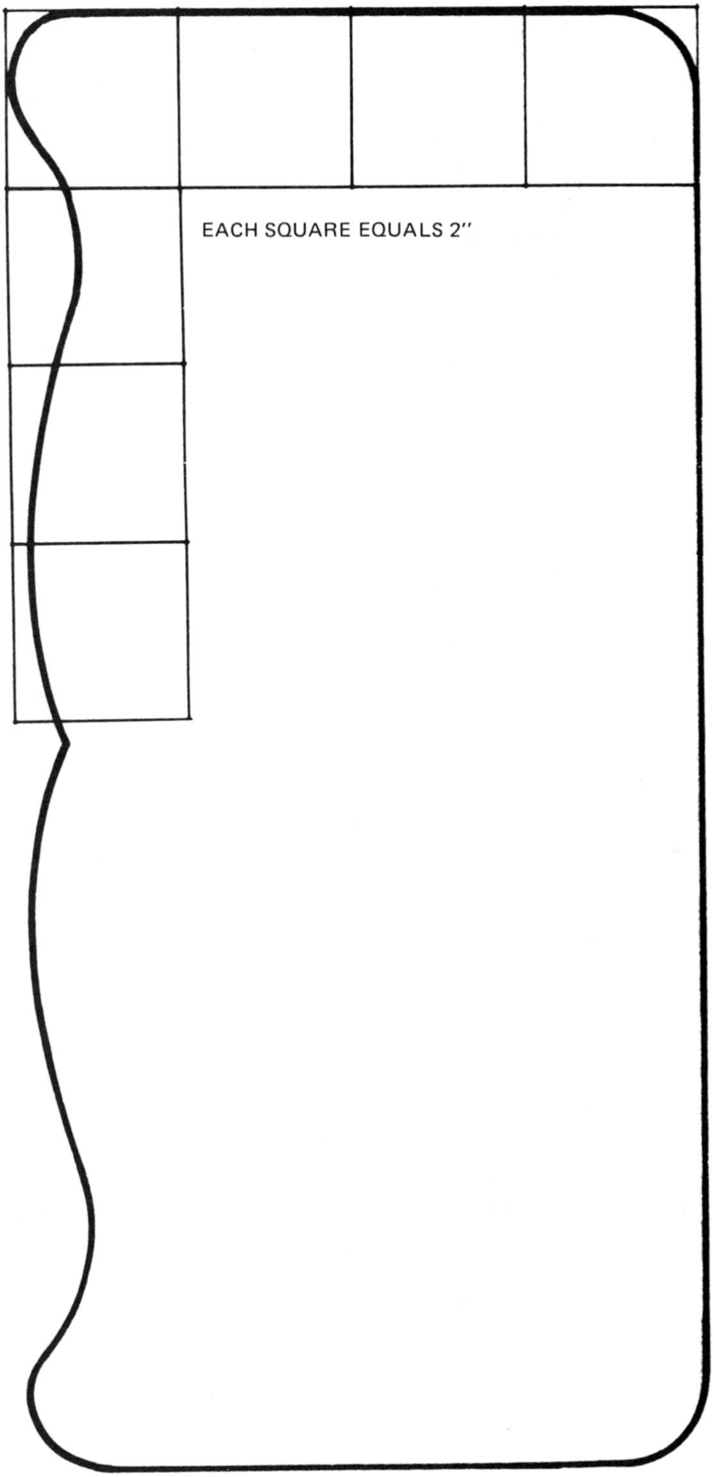

EACH SQUARE EQUALS 2″

1″ SQUARES

Fig. 7–19

TRESTLE TABLE

This small trestle table is a copy of its larger counterpart, which is usually used as a dining table. The two stretchers have been angled and serve as a trough for books. The table is ideally suited for use in the den, living room, or bedroom.

The 1-1/8-inch thick pine gives it a husky, sturdy appearance. The top, side, and base pieces are made of glued-up stock. To prevent warping, the annular rings should be alternated when gluing. Dowels are recommended for these joints, three in each end piece, and four at each joint along the length of the top. Dowels are not needed for the base pieces. Except for the pegs, all joints are fastened with lag screws.

Shaped parts are cut on the band saw or with a saber saw fitted with a long blade. The mortise for the tenons must be carefully cut so that they are straight and square. Usually such cuts go "off" because the tool is fed too fast or the blade is dull. The top and bottom edges of the end pieces must be squared up before the contours are cut. The radial arm saw should be used if available.

The three-quarter-inch-diameter holes for the pegs are set back slightly toward the shoulder. About one-sixteenth of an inch should suffice to permit the ends to come up tight against the shoulders of the stretcher. The ends of the pegs are rounded so they may be started into the holes.

Before assembly, all parts are rounded with a router. If a worn look is desired, a rasp or surform tool is used. The corners of the top are usually excessively worn in tables of this type. Excess wood may be removed with a spokeshave, and then the parts are finished with sandpaper.

Except for the glue used to make up the wide boards, no glue is needed in assembly. Lag screws are used throughout. Flat washers placed under the screw heads prevent the wood from being crushed.

Fig. 7-20 A spade bit is used to bore large holes for lag screw head and washer.

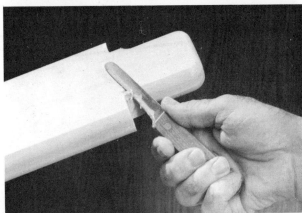

Fig. 7-21 A knife is used to whittle a square edge left by the router.

Fig. 7-22 Driving the pegs draws the legs tight against the stretcher.

Fig. 7-23 The legs are
fastened to a cleat with
lag screws. Using a ratchet
wrench saves time.

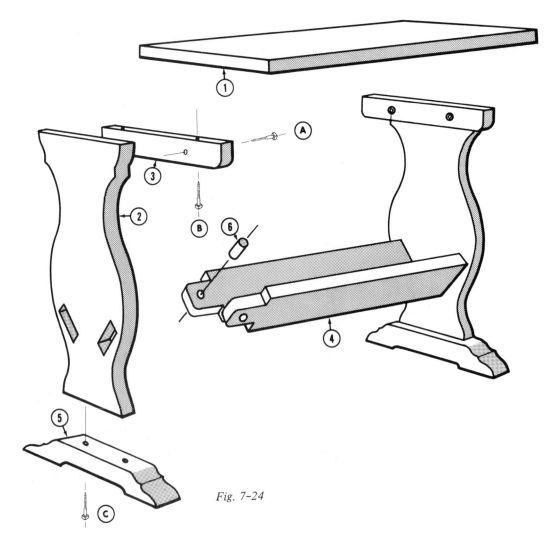

Fig. 7-24

Materials List for Trestle Table

Part	Description	Size and Material	Quantity
1	Top	1-1/8 × 18 × 28 pine	1
2	End	1-1/8 × 12 × 19-1/8 pine	2
3	Cleat	1-1/8 × 1-3/4 × 15-1/2 pine	2
4	Stretcher	1-1/8 × 4-1/2 × 26 pine	2
5	Base	2-1/4 × 2-1/4 × 16 pine	2
6	Peg	3/4 × 2-1/2 maple	4
A	Lag screw	5/16 × 2	4
B	Lag screw	5/16 × 2-1/2	6
C	Lag screw	5/16 × 3	4

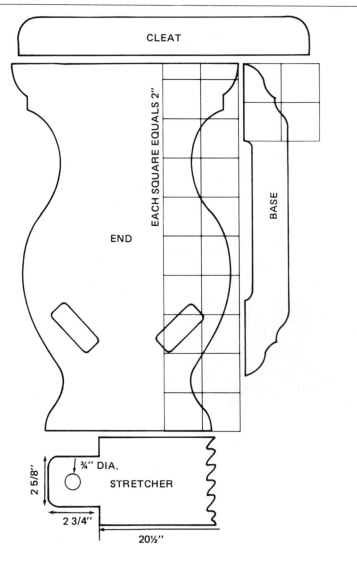

Fig. 7-25

TODDLER'S LOVE SEAT

Designed to please the younger set, the toddler's love seat is sturdily built of 1-1/8-inch pine and will take plenty of punishment. Buttons and plugs add to its attractive appearance.

To construct, the parts are laid out and cut as indicated. Then the screw shank, button, and plug holes are bored, with the larger ones being cut first, and then the shank holes. The holes for the buttons and plugs are the same size —five-sixteenths of an inch deep and one-half inch in diameter. The screws at the rear of the seat enter the backrest angularly, so they must be kept toward the rear edge.

The feet position is located on the skirt by drawing lines on the inner face of the skirts. These marks are indicated on the graph drawing.

Except for the end pieces, butt joints are used throughout. The end pieces are rabbeted along the lower and rear edges. Because of the width of the rabbet, it is best done on the table saw. The vertical passes are made first. Then the fence and depth of cut are reset, and with the work lying flat, the rabbet is cleaned out. The operator should keep fingers away from the blade and stand aside of the line of cut, as the waste will probably be thrown back toward him.

Fig. 7-26 The seat back being sanded after the edges have been heavily "worn" with a rasp.

All exposed edges are rounded with a router using a half-inch rounding bit. Then, using a rasp, heavy wear areas are made on the backrest, front of the seat, and ends of the armrests. The rasping is followed with medium and then fine sandpaper. All parts are assembled with screws and glue, except at the lower rabbet and between the skirt and feet, where screws only should be used. A shallow, tufted cushion adds nicely to this piece.

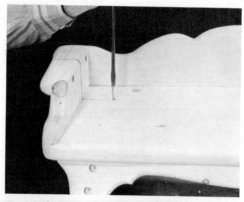

Fig. 7-27 Fastening seat assembly to the feet with flat-head screws.

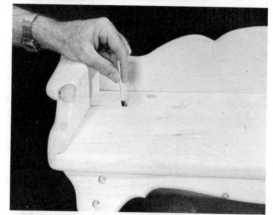

Fig. 7-28 Applying glue to the edge of a plug hole.

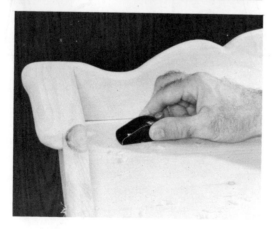

Fig. 7-29 Plugs are first surfaced with a small plane and then sanded.

Materials List for Toddler's Love Seat

Part	Description	Size and Material	Quantity
1	Backrest	1-1/8 × 4-1/2 × 24 pine	1
2	Seat	1-1/8 × 12 × 24 pine	1
3	Skirt	1-1/8 × 3-1/4 × 24-1/4 pine	2
4	Feet	1-1/8 × 8 × 10-3/4 pine	2
5	End	1-1/8 × 3-3/4 × 12-1/2 pine	2
6	Armrest	1-1/8 × 1-5/8 × 9 pine	2
A	Screw	2–10 FH	6
B	Screw	1-1/2 – 10 FH – 1/2″ plugs	13
C	Screw	2 – 10 FH – 5/8″ buttons	8

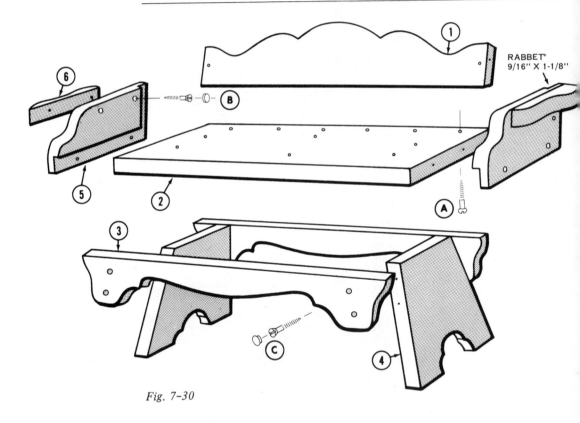

Fig. 7–30

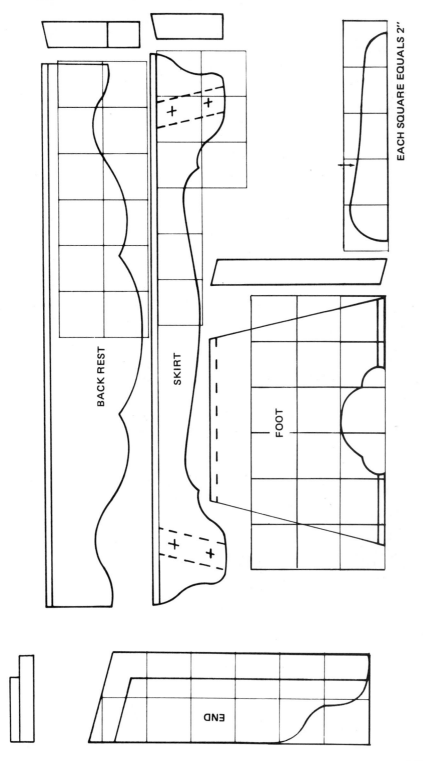

BACK REST

SKIRT

FOOT

END

EACH SQUARE EQUALS 2"

Fig. 7-31

HASSOCK BENCH

Made of poplar, this portable little bench doubles as a hassock. It has a padded cushion and heart-shaped hand holes at each end. Doweled joints eliminate the need for screws and plugs in the end pieces.

The parts are cut with a saber saw, and all exposed edges rounded with a 3/8 rounding bit fitted to the router.

The cleats are made a trifle shorter than the skirts. The vertical and horizontal screw clearance holes are drilled in the cleats first. Then the cleats are centered lengthwise on the skirts and installed with glue and screws.

The dowel holes in the skirt ends should penetrate 1-1/2-inches. This will leave 1/2 of an inch projecting for the end panels. If carefully laid out, the dowels should line up. However, the use of dowel centers will simplify this operation and ensure accuracy.

The bench top may be padded with foam and covered with upholstery vinyl, or a cushion may be sewed to fit.

Fig. 7-32 A jig block may be used to transfer dowel hole centers from the skirt to the end.

Fig. 7-33 *A router mounted upside down is used to round the edges of the end piece. A ball-bearing pilot prevents burn marks on wood.*

Materials List for Hassock Bench

Part	Description	Size and Material	Quantity
1	Top	1/2 X 8-1/8 X 17-3/4 plywood	1
2	End	13/16 X 10-3/4 X 12-3/4 poplar	2
3	Skirt	13/16 X 4-1/2 X 18 poplar	2
4	Cleat	3/4 X 1-5/8 X 17-7/8 pine	2

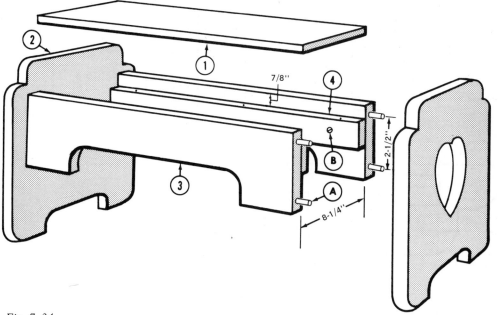

Fig. 7-34

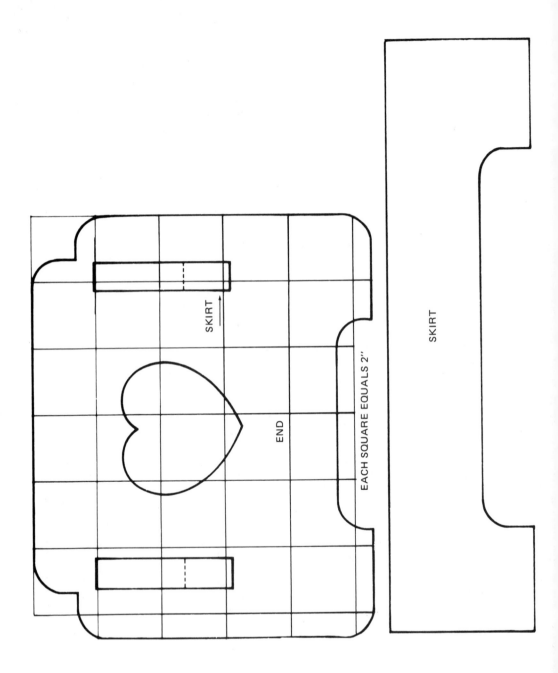

SKIRT

END

EACH SQUARE EQUALS 2"

SKIRT

172

Fig. 7–35

BOOK CASE

This attractive book case will make a fine addition to a study, living room, or bedroom. It is fairly simple to build and is a good exercise in making dadoes.

The boards are ripped to size, with the shelves cut three-eighths of an inch narrower than the sides to allow for the rabbet. The dadoes in the side pieces are made with the router or on the table saw. If the router is used, it is advantageous to cut both sections at one time to ensure that the dadoes will be perfectly aligned. The pieces are fastened firmly to a flat surface, the position of the dadoes is laid out, and a straightedge is clamped to the work, allowing the proper clearance for the router base. Unless a hardwood is being used, the 3/8-inch-deep cut may be made in one pass. The tool should be fed slowly, and the base kept solidly against the straightedge.

After the dadoes are cut, the back edges of the side pieces are rabbeted. Then the curved sections are laid out and cut with a saber saw. The subtop is ripped to size after the sides are completed. The widths of both must match.

Before assembling the parts, a router with a rounding bit is used to round all exposed edges. The router must not be run through the dadoes, but should be stopped just short of them. Likewise, the rounding of the shelves should cease three-eighths of an inch from the ends. Failure to do so will leave a gap at these points when the parts are assembled.

The screw and button holes are bored as required and then the pieces are assembled with glue and screws. Shelf ends should be glue-sized beforehand. The screws in the base piece are angled slightly into the end pieces. The ends and front base piece are fastened with 1-1/4-inch FH screws driven from the inside. The base should be installed so that its upper edge is 1/16 of an inch above the bottom edge of the bottom shelf.

The subtop is fastened to the sides using two-inch finishing nails driven from the topside into the rabbet. The top is added last, with screws driven up through the underside of the subtop. The back panel is installed with one-inch brads.

Fig. 7-36 *For greater accuracy, both side pieces are dadoed together.*

Materials List for Book Case

Part	Description	Size and Material	Quantity
1	Side	3/4 × 9 × 42-1/4 pine	2
2	Back	1/4 × 34 × 40-1/4 plywood	1
3	Top	3/4 × 8-1/2 × 36-1/4 pine	1
4	Subtop	3/4 × 7-1/4 × 33-1/4 pine	1
5	Skirt	3/4 × 2-3/4 × 35-1/2 pine	1
6	Shelf	3/4 × 8-3/4 × 34 pine	3
7	Base	3/4 × 4 × 36-1/4 pine	1
8	Apron	3/4 × 2 × 33-1/4 pine	1
9	End	3/4 × 4 × 9 pine	2
10	Base, rear	3/4 × 3-15/16 × 33-1/4 pine	1
A	Screw	1-1/2 – 8 FH – 5/8" button	16
B	Screw	1-1/4 – 8 FH	4

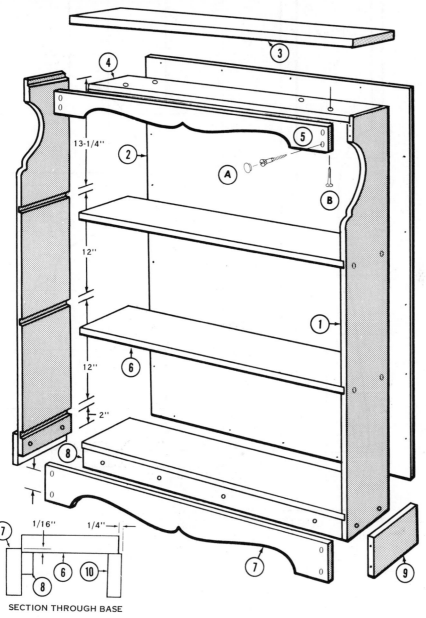

SECTION THROUGH BASE

Fig. 7-37

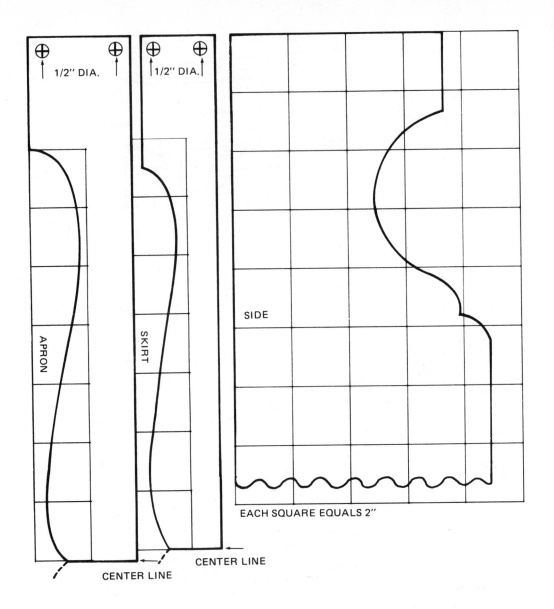

1/2" DIA.

1/2" DIA.

APRON

SKIRT

SIDE

EACH SQUARE EQUALS 2"

CENTER LINE

CENTER LINE

176

Fig. 7–38

SPLAYED LEG NIGHT TABLE

This early American night table is an excellent project for the beginner. Screwed butt joints and leg mounting brackets simplify construction. Buttons conceal the screws and add a decorative touch to the piece. This simple table is made of common pine and only a few basic tools are needed. The more advanced worker may prefer to use blind dadoes for fastening the shelves. If so, the shelf lengths should be increased accordingly.

The parts are laid out and cut to size. Then edges are rounded with a router. If a worn, distressed effect is desired, the edges may be shaped with a rasp, or file, as outlined in Chapter 6.

The rear edge of the side panels is rabbeted three-eighths of an inch by 3/4 of an inch to take the back panel. The screw shank and button holes are bored carefully, then the parts are assembled with glue and 1-1/2-inch FH screws. The end-grain screws should not be overtightened; when they bottom, the driving should stop.

The legs are cut from 1-3/4-inch stock. They may be tapered by hand with a plane or on the table saw using a tapering jig. After the tapers are cut, the center of the top edges is located, and a hole is bored for a hanger bolt. The size of the hanger bolt used depends on the mounting brackets to be installed. Some have two mountings—one for straight legs, the other for splayed legs. The single-splayed type should be purchased, as the double unit will not work on this table.

The threaded portion of the leg is inserted into the plate and tightened firmly. The leg must be positioned properly on the plate. The bottom end of the leg is sanded or cut to match the slope formed by the mounting plate. The legs are then fastened to the bottom shelf with three-quarter-inch roundhead screws.

The drawer is made as indicated in the drawing.

Fig. 7-39 A table saw was used to taper the leg, which can also be tapered with a hand plane.

Materials List for Splayed-Leg Night Table

Part	Description	Size and Material	Quantity
1	Side	3/4 × 10-3/4 × 19-1/2 pine	2
2	Back	3/4 × 13 × 20-1/2 pine	1
3	Shelf upper	3/4 × 5-3/4 × 12-1/4 pine	1
4	Shelf middle	3/4 × 9-1/4 × 12-1/4 pine	1
5	Shelf bottom	3/4 × 11-3/8 × 15 pine	1
6	Leg	1-3/4 × 1-3/4 × 8-3/4 pine	4
7	Drawer front	3/4 × 3-7/8 × 12-1/8 pine	1
8	Drawer rear	1/2 × 3 × 11-5/8 pine	1
9	Drawer side	1/2 × 3-1/2 × 8-3/4 pine	2
10	Drawer bottom	1/4 × 8-1/4 × 11-5/8 plywood	1
A	Screw	2 – 10 FH	9
B	Screw	1-1/2 – 10 FH – 5/8" buttons	18
C	Angular mounting plate		4
D	Screw for plate	1/2 – 8 RH	16

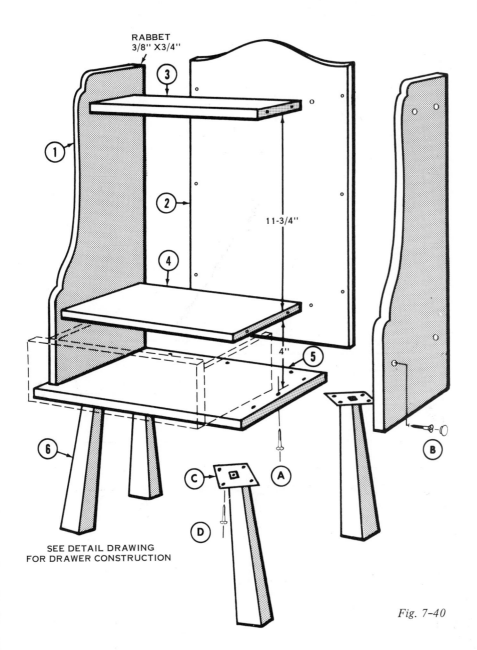

RABBET
3/8" X3/4"

11-3/4"

4"

SEE DETAIL DRAWING
FOR DRAWER CONSTRUCTION

Fig. 7-40

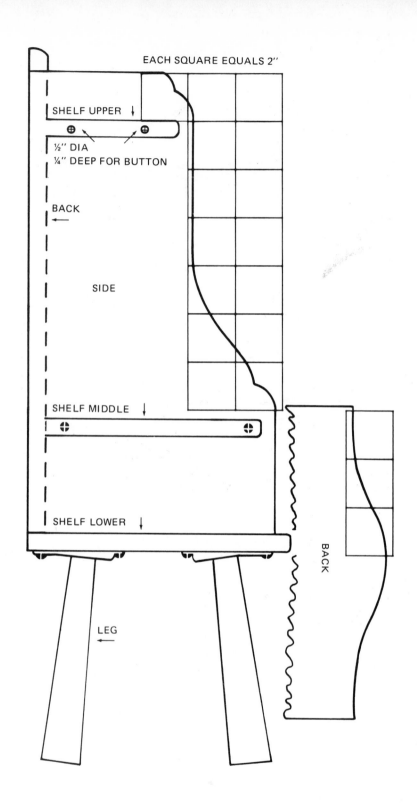

EACH SQUARE EQUALS 2"

SHELF UPPER

½" DIA
¼" DEEP FOR BUTTON

BACK

SIDE

SHELF MIDDLE

SHELF LOWER

LEG

BACK

Fig. 7-41

CRADLE MAGAZINE RACK

Utilizing barrel-making techniques in its construction, this novel cradle may be used for storing magazines, newspapers, or even logs. The staves are dadoed and made to fit around the curved ends. The sides of each stave are slightly beveled to produce a hairline joint when assembled.

Using eight, ten, or twelve-inch boards, the stock for the staves is cut to length, and the dadoes are made three-quarters of an inch from each end. The fence of the table saw is set at thirteen-sixteenths of an inch from the blade, and the required number of staves are then ripped. A few extra pieces should be made to avoid resetting the tools in the event of running short. After the strips are cut, the saw blade is set at an angle of four degrees; then both edges of each piece are ripped again. The fence is reset carefully so no stock is removed from the top surface of the staves when beveling. Since the pieces are narrow, a push stick should be used to keep the fingers safely away from the blade.

The strips are assembled with glue and 1-1/2-inch finishing nails. The glue is applied to the dadoes and along the edges. The first and last strip are surface nailed, and the rest are blind nailed edge to edge.

About five strips before the last stave is installed, the strips should be dry fit without nails to determine where the last piece ends. The last piece should stop at the shoulder. If necessary, the edge of one or more intermediate pieces may be trimmed to ensure that the last one will line up with the shoulder.

The four surface nails are then sunk and filled, and the feet are mounted with flathead screws.

Fig. 7-42 A dadoed board is ripped into strips on the table saw.

Fig. 7-43 The saw blade is tilted four degrees, and strips are recut to form a bevel.

Materials List for Cradle Magazine Rack

Part	Description	Size and Material	Quantity
1	End	3/4 × 10 × 13-3/4 pine	2
2	Stave	3/4 × 13/16 × 25 pine	30
3	Feet	3/4 × 2-3/8 × 12 pine	2
A	Finishing nail	1-1/2″	120
B	Screw	2-1/2 – 10 FH	4

182

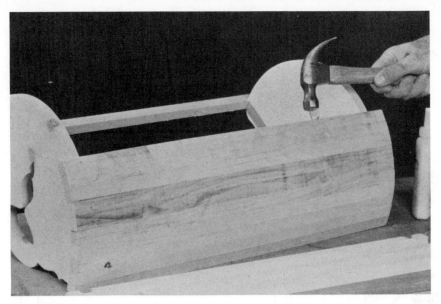

Fig. 7-44 Strips are glued and nailed edgewise with annular-ring paneling nails.

Fig. 7-45 The final strip (or strips) may have to be trimmed to fit.

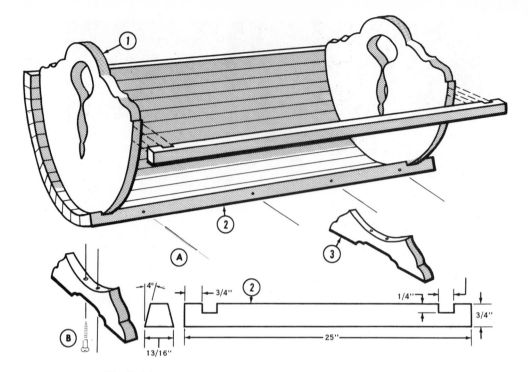

Fig. 7-46

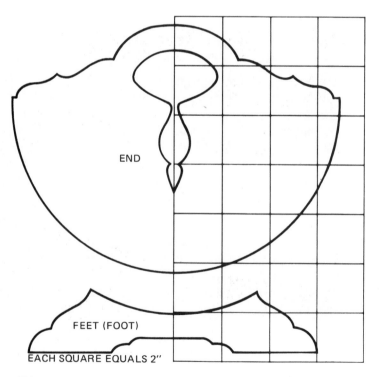

END

FEET (FOOT)

EACH SQUARE EQUALS 2"

Fig. 7–47

PLANTER WITH BOOK RACK

Made of pine boards, this planter provides an excellent project for the beginner using power tools, as it requires the use of the saber saw, router, drill, and table saw. The table saw is not essential, however, as the saber saw or portable saw may substitute for it.

The hand-hole and cloverleaf cutouts in the end pieces are made with the saber saw. A quarter-inch-diameter entry hole is bored in the waste area of each end piece. Then a fine-toothed blade is inserted for a smooth cut, which eliminates a lot of hand sanding later.

The holes for the buttons and screws are made next. With a spur or spade bit, the button holes are made one-half of an inch in diameter and five-sixteenths of an inch deep. The screw shank holes should be made three-sixteenths of an inch in diameter.

Before the lower edge is shaped, the skirts are grooved with the router or on the table saw. The groove should be placed 1-1/4 inches from the lower edge.

The lower shelf is made by screwing the two sections at right angles to each other and using three screws, glue, and plugs. Plug holes are bored five-sixteenths of an inch deep and one-half of an inch in diameter.

All edges, except the ends of the skirts and shelves, are rounded with a quarter-inch or three-eighths-inch rounding bit. To simplify the assembly of the lower shelves, a jig is cut from scrap as indicated and used to position the shelf relative to the lower edge of the side pieces. The planter bottom is inserted into the grooves and allowed to float without screws or glue.

Decals are optional. If they are used, the wood finish must be thoroughly dry before applying. Decals should not be used on shellacked surfaces.

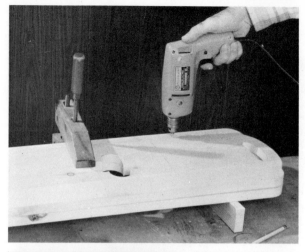

Fig. 7-48 End panels are clamped together to assure alignment of screw holes.

Fig. 7-49 Cutting a groove into the front panel on a table saw. A router may also be used for this step.

Fig. 7-50 A jig cut from scrap aids in aligning the lower shelf assembly.

Materials List for Planter with Book Rack

Part	Description	Size and Material	Quantity
1	End	3/4 X 10-3/8 X 32 pine	2
2	Skirt	3/4 X 8-1/2 X 34 pine	2
3	Planter bottom	3/4 X 8-1/2 X 34 pine	1
4	Shelf bottom	3/4 X 6-3/8 X 34 pine	1
5	Shelf rear	3/4 X 7-3/4 X 34 pine	1
A	Screw	1-1/2 – 8 FH – 5/8" buttons (20)	24

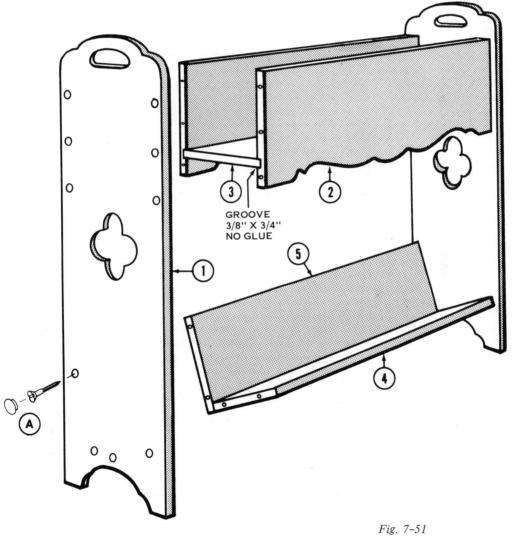

GROOVE
3/8" X 3/4"
NO GLUE

Fig. 7-51

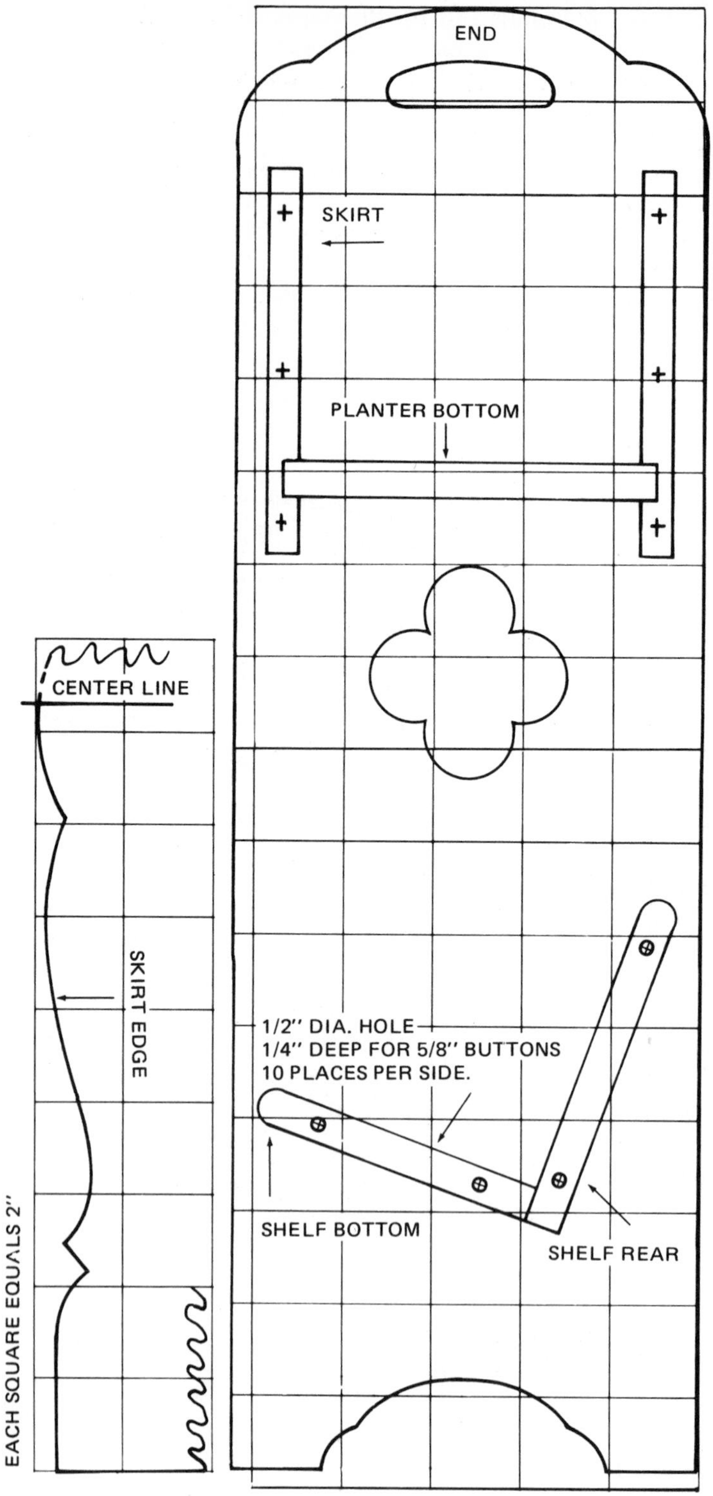

END

SKIRT

PLANTER BOTTOM

CENTER LINE

SKIRT EDGE

EACH SQUARE EQUALS 2"

1/2" DIA. HOLE
1/4" DEEP FOR 5/8" BUTTONS
10 PLACES PER SIDE.

SHELF BOTTOM

SHELF REAR

Fig. 7-52

CHAIR

As a rule, chairs are not easy to build, but this one is. Made of cherry lumber, a set of these will make a fine addition to a dining room. The seat and back are padded with foam for comfort. A chair of this type should be made of hardwood for sturdiness. Cherry was selected for the unit shown, but other species of hardwood may be substituted.

The parts are laid out and cut to size, with particular attention paid to the mating parts of the side members. These must be straight and square, and the dowel holes must be carefully aligned.

The chair is made of one-inch hardwood which actually measures thirteen-sixteenths of an inch. When laying out the parts, the following should be noted: the grain direction of each piece, that the side pieces are not square, and that the lengths of the upper and lower pieces are not equal. Shaped parts may be cut with a jigsaw, band saw, or saber saw. After cutting, all edges are sanded to remove saw marks.

The dowel holes in the side pieces are then located and drilled. The three-eighths-inch diameter holes are drilled perpendicular to the short edge of the stock. A doweling jig is very helpful here. After the holes are made, they are transferred to the vertical members using dowel centers.

Before assembling the sides, the end grain of the side pieces is glue-sized. Then it is recoated with glue, the dowels are inserted, and the parts are assembled. Wood pads are used to protect the work which is clamped securely. After the clamps are removed, a belt sander is run over the surface to level all of the joints.

The crosspieces are ripped to size, and then the ends are trimmed to length. The end cuts are beveled five degrees. Again, using a doweling jig, two dowel holes, 1-1/2 inches deep, are bored into the ends of each piece. The top edge of each piece is beveled five degrees, and the decorative groove is run along the lower edge of the front piece.

The next operation must be done with care. The position of the front and rear crosspieces are laid out onto the inner faces of the side members. A rectangle representing the cross section of these pieces is drawn. Before laying out the hole locations, tracing paper is used to check that the layout of the small rectangles in both the left and right side frames are in alignment. The frame is placed onto a sheet of tracing paper, and its outline is traced with a pencil. Then the paper is put on top of the frame and the traced line is registered to the frame. The two rectangles are drawn onto the paper, and then the tracing paper is flopped over again registering the outline of the frame. The small rectangles should line up; if not the cause of the error must be found and corrected. Dowel centers are used to transfer the hole positions onto the side frames.

Boring the holes in the side frames must be done at an angle of five degrees, which may easily be performed by using a simple jig which is shaped like an inverted *T*. The bottom edge of the jig is beveled five degrees after a guide hole has been bored through the upright of the *T*. The hole near the lower edge of the jig serves to admit light to permit visual centering of the jig over the laid out hole centers. In use, the jig is clamped in position while the holes are bored. A tape marker may be put on the drill to serve as a depth gauge. The holes should be bored one-half of an inch deep.

After the holes are bored, the edges of all of the members are rounded with a router fitted with a rounding cutter. The size of the round is optional; a quarter-inch bit was used here. The ends of the front and rear pieces are glue-sized, then joined with two-inch dowels and clamped securely.

The backrest pieces are laid out to size with the ends swayed back five degrees. However, it is best to cut the ends square about 1/4 of an inch longer than the actual size needed to permit boring of the dowel holes parallel to the sides or length of the piece. The 3/8-inch diameter holes are bored 1-3/4 inches

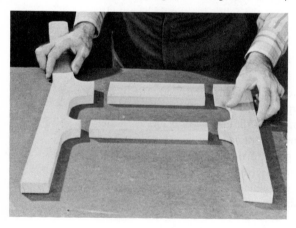

Fig. 7–53 Side parts are checked for fit after cutting.

deep using the doweling jig. After the holes are drilled, the ends are trimmed on the angular line laid out previously. The 1/4-inch by 1/4-inch groove is cut and the edges—*not* the ends—of both pieces are rounded off.

The quarter-inch plywood back panel is cut to size and fit into the grooved pieces. Following the procedure used for locating the crosspieces, the centers are marked for the dowels and then bored using the special jig.

Fig. 7-54 The doweling jig may be used for boring holes into the leg members.

Fig. 7-55 Pressure must be applied equally to both clamps to prevent uneven joints.

Fig. 7-56 A boring jig is used to bore angular holes in the frame.

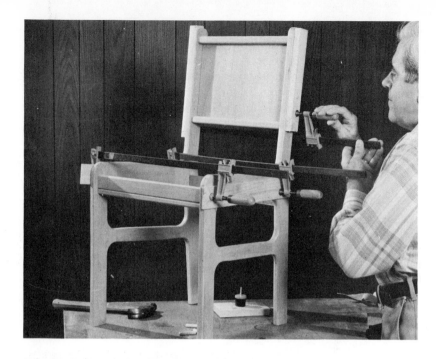

Fig. 7-57 Final assembly using small bar clamps at each doweled joint.

Materials List for Chair

Part	Description	Size and Material	Quantity
1	Leg, front	13/16 × 3-1/2 × 18 cherry	2
2	Leg, rear	13/16 × 5-1/2 × 33 cherry	2
3	Side, lower	13/16 × 1-1/2 × 10 cherry	2
4	Side, upper	13/16 × 2-7/8 × 9-7/8 cherry	2
5	Skirt, front	13/16 × 2-1/8 × 15-1/2 cherry	1
6	Skirt, rear	13/16 × 2-1/8 × 13-1/8 cherry	1
7	Brace, rear	13/16 × 6 × 6 oak	2
8	Brace, front	13/16 × 6 × 6 oak	2
9	Back support, lower	13/16 × 1-5/8 × 13-1/4 cherry	1
10	Back support, upper	13/16 × 1-5/8 × 13-1/4 cherry	1
11	Back	1/4 × 8-7/8 × 13-1/8 plywood	1
12	Seat	1/2 × 14-3/4 × 15-5/8 plywood	1
13	Urethane foam seat	2 × 14-3/4 × 15-5/8 foam	1
14	Urethane foam back	2 × 8-3/8 × 13-1/8 foam	1
15	Plasticized fabric		1 yd.
A	Dowel	3/8 × 2	24
B	Screw	1-1/4 – 8 FH	4
C	Screw	2-1/2 – 10 FH	8

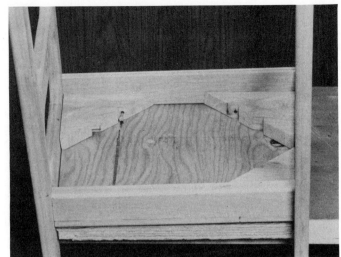

Fig. 7-58 An underside view of the chair shows how braces are installed.

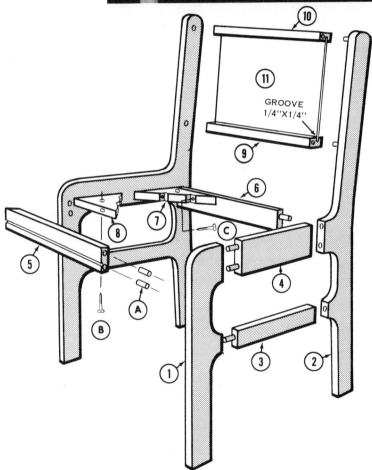

GROOVE
1/4"X1/4"

Fig. 7-59

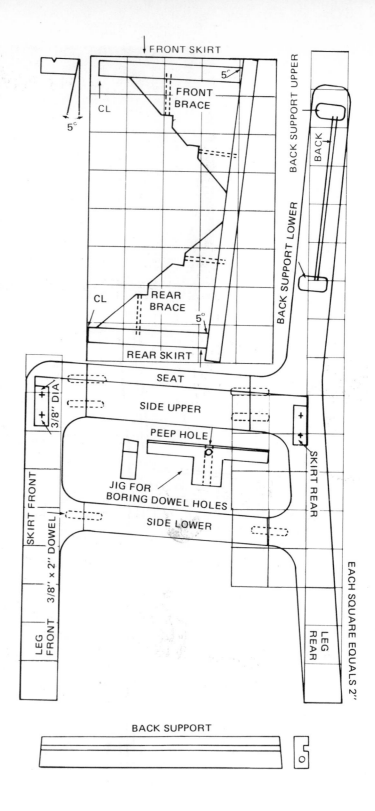

FRONT SKIRT

5°

FRONT
BRACE

CL

5°

BACK SUPPORT UPPER

BACK

BACK SUPPORT LOWER

CL

REAR
BRACE

5°

REAR SKIRT

SEAT

SIDE UPPER

3/8" DIA

PEEP HOLE

SKIRT REAR

JIG FOR
BORING DOWEL HOLES

SIDE LOWER

SKIRT FRONT

3/8" x 2" DOWEL

LEG
FRONT

LEG
REAR

EACH SQUARE EQUALS 2"

BACK SUPPORT

Fig. 7-60

CONTEMPORARY DINING TABLE

The modern look is quite apparent in this attractive streamlined dining table. The beauty of this piece lies in its simplicity of style and construction. All of its members are made of birch kitchen cabinet framing, which is stocked by most lumberyards. Used primarily for the rails and stiles of kitchen cabinets, they are available in two sizes: 13/16 by 2-13/16 inches and 13/16 by 3 inches. The lengths are random size.

Since the stock need not be ripped to width, construction is fast. The various pieces are cut to length, then the dowel holes are bored, two at each joint. Using a doweling jig is recommended; if not available, however, dowel centers may be used to locate the holes in the mating pieces. With a drill press, a simple jig may be made consisting of a backstop and end guide. This takes care of all of the cross-grain holes. The end-grain holes have to be made with the dowel jig or by hand. All of the holes must be bored straight.

A splined joint is used at the inside edge of each frame section. The bevels and spline are cut after the dowel holes are bored but before assembly. The table saw blade is tilted at an angle of thirty degrees, then the fence is set to produce the double bevel in each of the six mating pieces.

Before cutting the work pieces, test cuts are made on scrap wood of the same thickness and width. The stock is fed through the saw flat to cut the first bevel. For the second pass, the piece is turned upside down.

The splines are cut by lowering the saw blade (still at the thirty-degree angle) and moving the fence as required. The work is now fed on edge. The first spline is cut, then the work is reversed and the second spline cut. A push stick should be used so that fingers are well away from the saw blade. The saw blade should produce a kerf to match the plywood spline (one-eighth of an inch).

Before assembling the frame sections the shank holes are bored for the mounting screws into the upper rail sections. Each frame section is glued up individually before joining the splines. Since one edge of the outer frames and both edges of the center frame are beveled, clamping pads must be made up to match the bevel. These are cut from scrap wood using the same saw setting utilized to cut the bevels. After the frames are glued, the lower corner of the outer frames is rounded off with a saber saw. This is followed with a good sanding and, if necessary, a scraping of the joints to level them. The pieces are dusted thoroughly, then all of the exposed corners are rounded off inside and out with a router. The splines are cut to fit, and the frames are then glued. Belt clamps hold the pieces while the glue sets.

The top consists of a rectangular frame similar to the lower ones, except that only the outer edges are rounded with the router. The top is made up of plastic laminate mounted to a plywood base. Since the underside of the top will be secured to the table frame, it is not necessary to add a backing laminate to the underside of the top. The top is cut to fit the frame snugly and held with screws driven diagonally through the top into the frame.

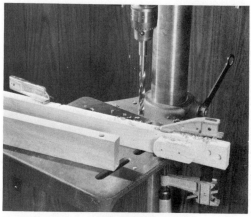

Fig. 7-61 A simple jig is used to bore dowel holes in stiles.

Fig. 7-62 Cutting splines into the inner rails.

Fig. 7-63 Inserting spiral groove
dowels into stiles.

Fig. 7-64 Glue-sizing the ends of
the rail pieces will prevent excess
absorption.

Fig. 7-65 A clamping block made from scrap.

Fig. 7–66 Two band clamps are sufficient for clamping stiles.

Materials List for Dining Table

Part	Description	Size and Material	Quantity
1	Top	3/4 X 26 X 56 fir plywood	1
2	Top, side	13/16 X 2 X 60 birch	2
3	Top, end	13/16 X 2 X 26 birch	2
4	Stile	13/16 X 2 X 28-1/2 birch	10
5	Rail, end	13/16 X 2 X 7-1/2 birch	8
6	Rail, center	13/16 X 2 X 26 birch	2
7	Spline	1/8 X 1/2 X 28-1/2 plywood	6
A	Screw	2-1/2 – 10 FH	10
B	Screw	1-1/4 – 8 RH	16

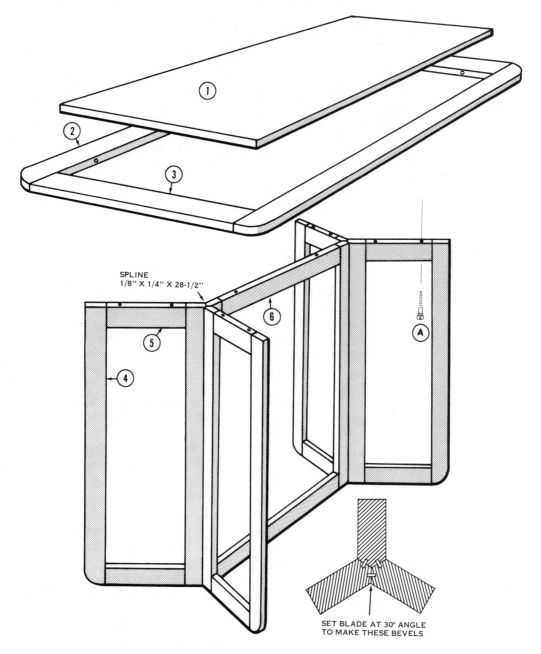

SPLINE
1/8'' X 1/4'' X 28-1/2''

SET BLADE AT 30° ANGLE
TO MAKE THESE BEVELS

Fig. 7-67

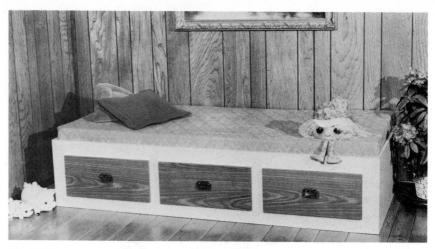

Fig. 7–68

BED WITH STORAGE

Made of plywood and plastic laminate, this sturdy bed has three roomy drawers for storage. The unit shown has a four-inch foam mattress, but a thicker one may be substituted.

Since the plywood will be covered with laminate, construction is somewhat simplified. Butt joints glued and nailed are easily made. Galvanized finishing nails have great holding power and are recommended instead of the usual bright finishing nails.

Time and effort may be saved by having the lumber dealer cut the large panels to size. If it is cut at home, a guide strip clamped to the work will ensure a straight, clean cut.

To save material, the three dropped-out panels for the drawer openings are used for the drawer fronts. They will have to be made larger however, by adding a strip along the bottom and end of each. This will not be objectionable, since the panels will be covered with laminate.

Before assembling the frame members, the edges of the end panels are glue-sized. The glue is allowed to dry for about ten minutes, and then the members are recoated and nailed with two-inch galvanized nails. Diagonal cleats hold the frame square while the glue sets.

The mattress board cleats must be installed accurately. This may be accomplished with a gauge block cut from scrap wood. The piece should be made exactly two inches wide and then used to position the cleats. The cleats are installed with glue and 1-1/4-inch nails. The mattress board supports are notched to fit around the cleats. They are shown upside down in the drawing. They should be inverted and installed between the cleat and drawer runners.

To ensure that the drawer runners are aligned, the upright supports are used as gauges before being fastened permanently to the crosspieces. The supports are placed along the bottom edge of the frame and the runners are rested on them. The center runner should project equally on both sides of the drawer opening when fastened to the frame. The upright supports are assembled and added last.

The laminate is applied as explained in Chapter 3. If the bed is to be used with a long side against a wall, the laminate may be eliminated from that side to keep costs down to a minimum.

Fig. 7-69 Lines for drawer cutouts are gauged with a combination square.

Fig. 7-70 A saber saw is used to drop the cutouts, and the waste is saved.

Fig. 7-71 A router is used to smooth the edges left by the saw.

Fig. 7-72 When assembling the bed frame, nails and glue should be used on all joints.

Fig. 7-73 Guides must be installed accurately to ensure proper operation of the drawers.

Fig. 7-74 Applying contact cement to the frame with a roller should be done outdoors if possible.

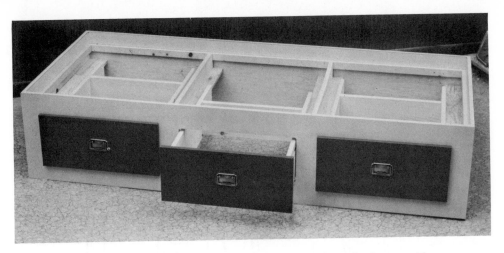

Fig. 7-75 A completed bed without mattress board. Note how the drawers ride on runners.

Materials List for Bed with Storage

Part	Description	Size and Material	Quantity
1	Front/rear	3/4 X 15-5/8 X 74 plywood	2
2	End	3/4 X 15-5/8 X 30-1/2 plywood	2
3	Runner center	3/4 X 4-5/8 X 30-1/2 plywood	2
3A	Runner end	3/4 X 3-3/4 X 30-1/2 plywood	2
4	Mattress board support	3/4 X 3 X 30-1/2 plywood	2
5	Crosspiece	3/4 X 2-1/8 X 30-1/2 pine	2
6	Upright support	3/4 X 3-5/8 X 9-1/2 pine	4
7	Cleat front/rear	3/4 X 1-1/4 X 72-1/2 pine	2
8	Cleat, end	3/4 X 1-1/4 X 29 pine	2
9	Mattress board	1/4 X 30-3/8 X 72-3/8 plywood	1
10	Drawer side	3/4 X 6-3/4 X 28 pine	6
11	Drawer back	3/4 X 6 X 18-1/4 pine	3
12	Drawer subfront	3/4 X 6-3/4 X 18-1/4 pine	3
13	Drawer front	3/4 X 8-1/4 X 20-3/4 plywood	3
14	Drawer bottom	1/4 X 18-1/4 X 20-3/8 plywood	3
15	Laminate		24 sq. ft.
	Nails, galvanized	2" finishing	

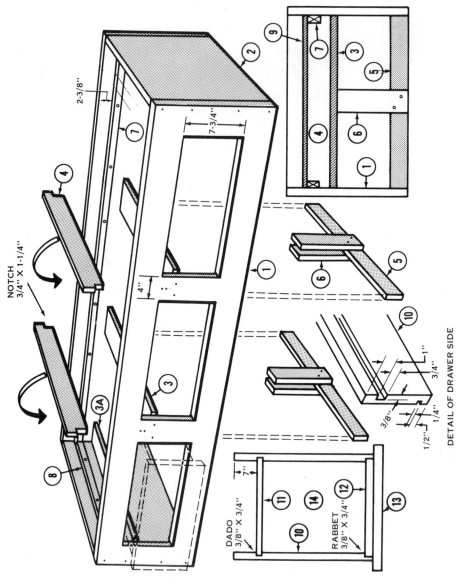

2-3/8"

7-3/4"

4"

NOTCH
3/4" X 1-1/4"

DETAIL OF DRAWER SIDE

1"

3/4"

3/8"

1/4"

1/2"

DADO
3/8" X 3/4"

7"

RABBET
3/8" X 3/4"

Fig. 7-76

Fig. 7-77

TELEPHONE STAND

This novel telephone table may also be used as a night table. The pivoted door rotates at a flick of the finger to reveal a telephone directory neatly stored on the back side. The interior provides ideal storage area. The table is covered with wood-grain laminate and trimmed with moldings for a raised panel effect. A set of ball casters make the unit mobile.

Fir plywood is used to form the boxlike structure. Before laying out the door cutout, the moldings should be on hand. Called *cabinet moldings,* they are available with premitered corner curves in various radii. The most commonly used is the provincial design in either the two- or three-inch radius. The straight sections of molding must be mitered to fit the curved sections. Because of the variations in widths available, sizes are not given in the drawing. The strips are mitered to make up the panel and placed onto a sheet of kraft paper. The inner edge of the moldings is then carefully traced. The pattern is cut and used to trace the shape of the door. The pattern should be saved for later, as it is used to position the moldings on the laminate surface. A blade entry hole is made along one of the straightedges, then the door opening is cut with a saber saw. The waste should be saved as it will become the door.

The "box" is assembled with glue and two-inch finishing nails. The joints are butted as indicated in the drawing.

The laminate is prepared by cutting the various panels one-quarter of an inch larger all around than the wood panels. Cement is applied to all of the laminate panels and to two opposite sides of the cabinet. After the cement has set, two of the laminate pieces are applied to the coated cabinet surfaces. A router fitted with a straight trimmer is used to trim the edges flush with the cabinet. Next, cement is applied to the two remaining sides of the cabinet and the procedure is repeated except that the router is now fitted with a bevel trimmer and used along the four vertical corners. The door is laminated next, and then the door opening and top edges are trimmed with a straight cutter. The cabinet top is laminated last and trimmed with the bevel cutter.

The book brackets are added to the back of the door with screws of suitable length that are spaced to suit the telephone directory to be used. The pivot hinges are designed to fit between the kerf cuts made by the saw. If necessary, the top and bottom edges of the door may be trimmed so that it will swing freely without binding. The flathead screws are positioned so that the pivot is perfectly centered.

The moldings are stained and finished to match the laminate. The back of the molding must be kept free of stain. The pattern is placed onto the cabinet sides, centered and straight. A narrow bead of white glue is applied to the back-side of the moldings, which are then pressed into place. Also, a bit of glue is added to the molding ends. If desired, contact cement may be used in place of the white glue.

The door and opening edges are glue-sized several times, then sanded lightly and painted with a matching or darker tone than the laminate. To complete, the wheels and pulls are added.

Fig. 7-78 A plywood cube is assembled with nails and glue.

Materials List for Telephone Stand

Part	Description	Size and Material	Quantity
1	Top/bottom	3/4 × 18 × 18 plywood	2
2	Side	3/4 × 16-1/2 × 16-1/2 plywood	2
3	End	3/4 × 16-1/2 × 18 plywood	2
4	Door	3/4 × 12-3/4 × 12-3/4 plywood	1
5	Molding	5/8" × 16' plus 16 corners	
6	Bracket	3/4 × 1 × 1-1/2 pine	2
7	Rail	1/4 × 1-1/2 × 10-1/2 pine	1
8	Tab	1/4 × 2-1/2 × 3 plywood	1
9	Book rest	3/4 × 3 × 1 pine	1
A	Nail	2" finishing	36
B	Pivot hinge		1
C	Ball casters		4
D	Laminate		16 sq. ft.

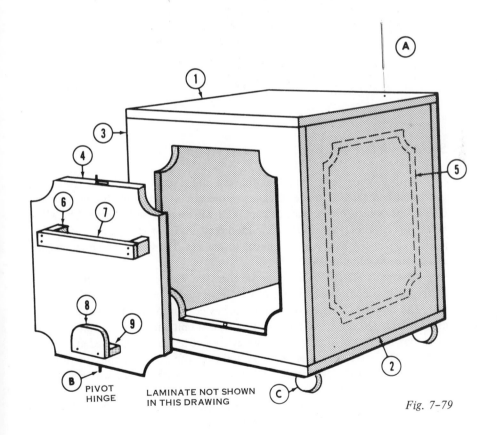

PIVOT HINGE   LAMINATE NOT SHOWN IN THIS DRAWING

Fig. 7–79

Fig. 7-80

SMALL END TABLE

With a convenient drawer at the top and a small shelf below for books, this small end table is made of lumber core birch, except for the top rail and base beads, which are poplar. Assembly is with screws and dowels. The screw holes for fastening the top are counterbored into the end panels, as are the screw holes in the base which connect to the legs. The shelf is tilted ten degrees and fastened with blind dowels.

The parts are cut to size, and the edges are shaped with a router. The back of the shelf is contoured so that it does not project past the leg outline at the rear. The dowel holes are bored 1-1/2 inches deep into the shelves and 1/2 inch into the legs. The lower section is assembled as a unit and then set aside.

For the top section, the rail pieces are cut to size and mitered at the back corners. The section is assembled as follows: top to rails, ends to top, and drawer support to ends. Finally, the lower subassembly is added. The drawer is made without guides or runners.

To prevent the end grain from absorbing too much finish, it should be sized moderately with highly diluted white glue or diluted sealer.

Fig. 7-81 The legs are cut out with a saber saw. The work is propped on blocks for blade clearance.

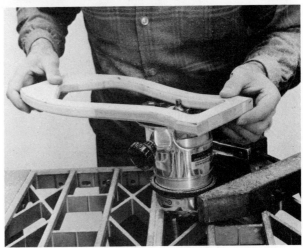

Fig. 7-82 Shaping edges with an inverted router. Clamps are used to hold the router firmly to the table.

Fig. 7-83 Feet are fastened to the legs through counterbored holes at the bottom.

Fig. 7-84 The ends and back panel are fastened to the top after the rails have been installed.

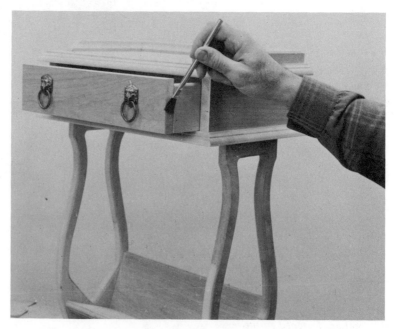

Fig. 7-85 Applying sealer to the end grain before applying stain.

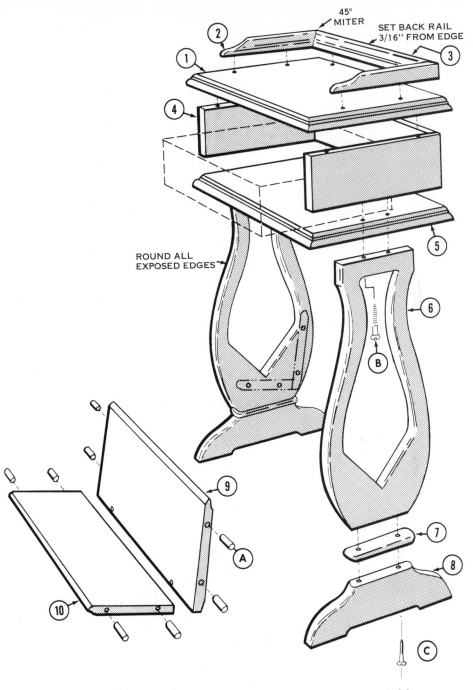

45°
MITER

SET BACK RAIL
3/16" FROM EDGE

ROUND ALL
EXPOSED EDGES

Fig. 7-86

211

Materials List for Small End Table

Part	Description	Size and Material	Quantity
1	Top	3/4 × 10-1/2 × 17 plywood	1
2	Rail end	3/4 × 1 × 8-1/16 poplar	2
3	Rail rear	3/4 × 1 × 15-5/8 poplar	1
4	End	3/4 × 3-1/4 × 9-5/8 plywood	2
5	Drawer support	3/4 × 10-1/2 × 17 plywood	1
6	Leg	3/4 × 7-3/8 × 16 plywood	2
7	Spacer	3/16 × 1 × 4-5/8 poplar	2
8	Feet	3/4 × 2-1/2 × 10-1/2 plywood	2
9	Shelf back	3/4 × 5-1/2 × 14-1/16 plywood	1
10	Shelf	3/4 × 4-1/2 × 14-1/16 plywood	1
11	Back panel	3/4 × 3-1/4 × 14-1/16 plywood	1
12	Drawer front	3/4 × 3-3/16 × 14 plywood	1
13	Drawer subfront	1/2 × 2-7/8 × 13-1/2 mahogany	1
14	Drawer rear	1/2 × 2-3/8 × 13-1/2 mahogany	1
15	Drawer side	1/2 × 2-7/8 × 8-1/16 mahogany	2
16	Drawer bottom	1/4 × 7-7/16 × 13-1/2 plywood	1
A	Dowel	3/8 × 2	8
B	Screw	2-1/2 – 8 FH	10
C	Screw	2 – 8 FH	4
D	Screw	1-1/4 – 8 FH	8

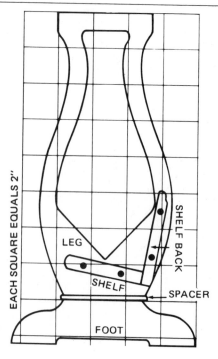

EACH SQUARE EQUALS 2"

LEG

SHELF BACK

SHELF

SPACER

FOOT

Fig. 7-87

TREASURE CHEST FOR TOYS

No book on woodworking would be complete without a treasure chest. Made of plywood, hardboard, and pine, this toy box may be used as a footlocker when the child outgrows the toy stage. The plywood and pine framework is covered with wood-grained hardboard. The banding and ornaments simulating metal are also cut from hardboard and are painted to resemble brass. The project takes half of a sheet of hardboard and about one-fourth of a sheet of plywood.

The plywood and pine framing are cut and assembled using two-inch finishing nails and glue. It should be noted that the rear framing strip is set below the frame sides to allow clearance for the hinge. The amount of setback is determined by measuring the thickness of the strip hinge in the closed position.

The wood-grained hardboard is cut to size and applied with glue and annular paneling nails which have excellent holding power. Glue is employed without nails along the top framing members which are not to be covered with trim. Clamps are used at these points.

The curved top is covered by applying one-inch strips of hardboard which are glued edge to edge. Nails are also used at the end and center bearing points. To secure a tight joint between the strips, the edges are beveled by setting the table saw blade at an angle of three degrees.

The lockplate, handles, and banding are cut from one-eighth-inch hardboard. Each part is fit individually, and the corners are mitered where necessary. Before installing these pieces, the surface is lightly scuffed with 6/0 paper and sprayed with bronze paint. The final trim consists of decorative upholstery tacks spaced as indicated in the photo. Swivel casters, hinge, and lid support complete the chest.

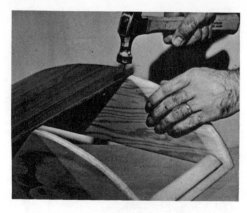

Fig. 7-88 A curved top is made from hardboard strips glued edge to edge and is nailed to the end pieces.

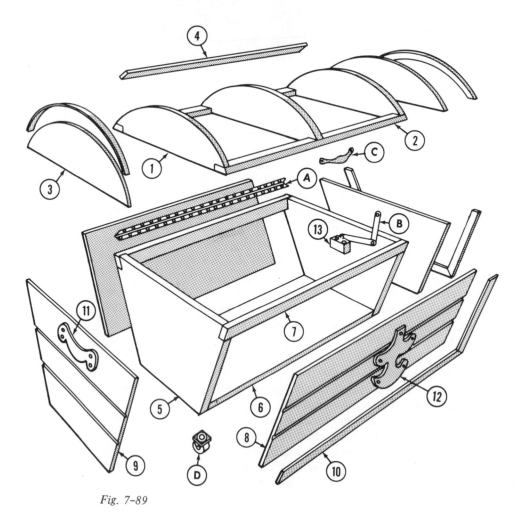

Fig. 7-89

Materials List for Treasure Chest

Part	Description	Size and Material	Quantity
1	Lid rib	3/4 X 4-3/4 X 18 plywood	3
2	Lid rail	3/4 X 2 X 26 pine	2
3	Lid end cover	1/4 X 5 X 18-1/2 hardboard	2
4	Lid cover	1/4 X 1 X 26 hardboard	24
5	Chest end	3/4 X 12-1/4 X 18 plywood	2
6	Chest bottom	3/4 X 10 X 24-1/2 plywood	1
7	Chest rail	3/4 X 1-1/2 X 26 pine	2
8	Chest cover	1/4 X 12-1/4 X 26 hardboard	2
9	Chest end cover	1/4 X 12-1/4 X 18-1/2 hardboard	2
10	Trim	1/8" X 1" hardboard	30 ft.
11	Handle	1/8 X 3 X 7 hardboard	1
12	Lockplate	1/8 X 7 X 10 hardboard	1
13	Lid support block	Size as required	2
A	Strip hinge	1-1/2" flat X 26"	1
B	Lid support	8"	2
C	Handle		1
D	Swivel caster		4

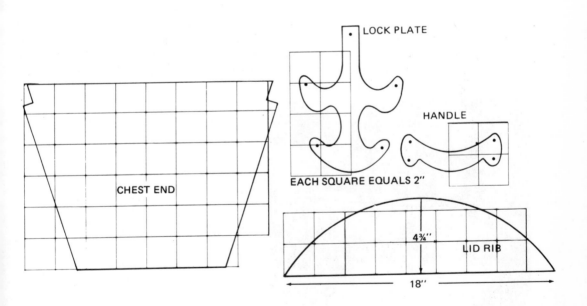

LOCK PLATE

HANDLE

EACH SQUARE EQUALS 2"

CHEST END

4¾"

LID RIB

18"

Fig. 7-90

SWAN ROCKER

Made of exterior-grade plywood, this toy is completely waterproof and may be left on the lawn as an ornament when not in use.

The design is first sketched onto kraft paper and cut out; then the outline is traced onto wood. If a band saw is used, two pieces of wood may be tacked together and both boards cut at the same time. Only one board should be cut at a time with a saber saw.

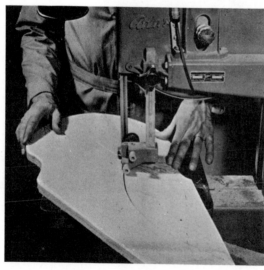

Fig. 7-91 All parts are cut from exterior-grade plywood. The edges must be sanded after sawing.

The parts are assembled with waterproof glue, screws, and plugs. All edges are sanded and rounded until glass-smooth. All exposed edges are glue-sized, and then an undercoater and several coats of exterior enamel are applied. The beak and wing details are added after the base coat dries.

For a smoother finish, MDO (medium density overlay) plywood may be preferred to fir plywood. This exterior-type plywood with a smooth, resin-treated surface takes paint beautifully. Costing slightly more than regular plywood, MDO plywood is a pleasure to work with and is ideal for outdoor furniture and built-ins. Most lumberyards carry MDO plywood or will order it for the customer.

Fig. 7-92 The rocker is assembled with waterproof glue and screws. To keep moisture out, the screws and plug are countersunk.

Materials List for Swan Rocker

Part	Description	Size and Material	Quantity
1	Side	3/4 × 22-1/2 × 50 plywood	2
2	Head	3/4 × 14 × 22-3/4 plywood	1
3	Front	3/4 × 14 × 11 plywood	1
4	Bottom	3/4 × 14 × 20 plywood	1
5	Seat	3/4 × 14 × 10-1/2 plywood	1
6	Back	3/4 × 14 × 11 plywood	1
A	Screw	1-1/2 – 8 FH – 1/2" plug	24

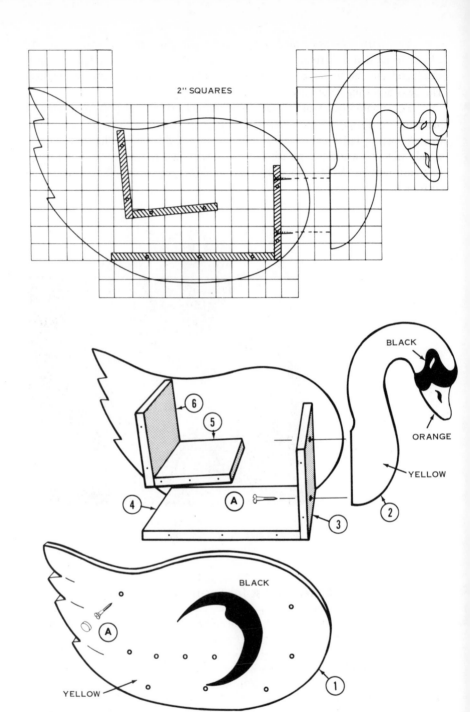

2'' SQUARES

BLACK

ORANGE

YELLOW

BLACK

YELLOW

Fig. 7-93

Fig. 7-94

CAMPAIGN STYLE DESK

Widely used in the past by British army officers while in the field in India, campaign desks were made with removable collapsible legs so that they could be transported easily. The corners of such desks (and chests) were usually reinforced with heavy brass trim to protect them. Nowadays, the trim is strictly decorative. The desk shown here has fixed legs and has been improved somewhat with the use of a tough plastic laminate.

Butt joints are used throughout to simplify construction. Also, fir plywood is used, as this will be covered with a laminate. However, if a wood finish is preferred, a better species of wood, such as lumber core birch or maple, should be chosen. Also, the top and bottom boards must be rabbeted and dadoed to receive the ends and dividers, and the width of the ends and dividers must be increased accordingly.

To further keep construction simple, the back panel is set back and nailed onto the cabinet. The advanced woodworker may prefer to set it flush, in which case the ends, top, and bottom should be rabbeted and the two dividers shortened one-fourth of an inch.

Glue and two-inch finishing nails are used to assemble the cabinet. To minimize absorption, which is considerable with plywood, all edges are glue-sized.

The laminate is applied to the top, ends, and front. The legs are painted, but there is no reason why they cannot be laminated, too, if one has the ambition. Since the corners will be concealed with hardware, the laminate may be applied to the front of the cabinet with butt joints. The laminate is cut in one-inch-wide strips, making the two long strips 53 inches in length. The divider strips are made 4-1/2 inches long. These are applied first, after they have been coated with contact cement. The strips are centered in length and width, then pressure is applied, as outlined in Chapter 3. The long pieces are attached next, and then all of the edges are trimmed flush. The end pieces are added and trimmed, and then the same is done with the top. When installing the brass trim, the clearance holes must be bored only through the laminate. These holes are made slightly larger than the diameter of the escutcheon pins. Nails or pins cannot be driven through undrilled laminate without cracking it.

The sawhorse legs are easily made, but care should be exercised when boring the dowel holes, which must be made fifteen degrees off of perpendicular. After boring the diagonal holes, the legs are fastened to the stretcher with three-eighths-inch spiral dowels. The long dowels are inserted, and then the upper part of the legs is glued and screwed to the crosspieces.

The drawers are constructed as indicated in the detail. The ends of the front panel are beveled to permit the drawer to close without binding. Also, beveling serves as a self-centering feature. After the front has been laminated and trimmed, the ends are beveled, because a router trimming bit can only be used on square edges. The bevel is run from the outside corner to the drawer side, which should be a total of one-sixteenth of an inch on each side.

Materials List for Campaign-Style Desk

Part	Description	Size and Material	Quantity
1	Top	3/4 X 19-3/4 X 52-11/16 plywood	1
2	Bottom	3/4 X 19-3/4 X 52-5/8 plywood	1
3	End	3/4 X 4-3/4 X 19-3/4 plywood	2
4	Divider	3/4 X 4-3/4 X 19-3/4 plywood	2
5	Leg	1-1/8 X 1-1/8 X 23-3/4 poplar	8
6	Stretcher	1-1/8 X 1-1/4 X 14 poplar	4
7	Dowel	3/4 X 10-1/2 maple	4
8	Crosspiece	1-3/4 X 2 X 16-1/4 poplar	2
9	Back	1/4 X 5-1/2 X 51-7/8 plywood	1
10	Drawer front	3/4 X 4-11/16 X 16-1/2 plywood	3
11	Drawer sub front	1/2 X 4-5/8 X 16-1/8 pine	3
12	Drawer back	1/2 X 4-1/8 X 16-1/8 pine	3
13	Drawer side	1/2 X 4-5/8 X 18-1/2 pine	6
14	Drawer bottom	1/4 X 16-1/8 X 17 plywood	3
15	Laminate (not illustrated)		12 sq. ft.
A	Screw	2-1/2 – 12 FH	4
B	Campaign hardware, corners, tees, and pulls		
C	Spiral dowel	3/8 X 2	8

Fig. 7-95 The leg assembly is fastened with glue and screws.

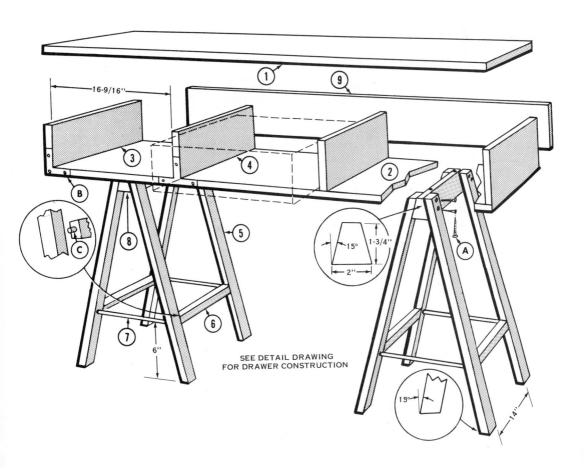

16-9/16"

1-3/4"

15°

2"

6"

SEE DETAIL DRAWING
FOR DRAWER CONSTRUCTION

15°

14"

Fig. 7-96

Fig. 7-97

ELEGANT COFFEE TABLE

Featuring tapestry prints on all four sides, this coffee table is uniquely different. If paintings or photographs are preferred, they may be used instead of the fabric.

Construction is begun by making two frames, each consisting of a skirt, inner base, and two corner posts. The screw shank holes are bored in the skirts and inner base pieces. The parts are assembled with nails and glue, with the nails placed where they are concealed by the moldings whenever possible. The basic frame is completed by adding the balance of the skirts and base pieces. The outer base pieces are mitered, splined, and then fastened to the inner base with screws and glue.

The moldings are cut next. There are three types of molding used: base, cove, and crown. The base and cove moldings are held flat when mitering; the crown molding must be held at the mounting angle. The base moldings are cut first. If the frame was accurately cut and assembled, a gauge is set and all horizontal members are cut 17 inches long, and all vertical members 16-3/8 inches long. If, however, discrepancies are apparent in the frame, each piece must be mitered and fit separately. The miters should be snug enough so only glue is needed to hold them in place. If nails are needed, they should be driven from inside of the cabinet. The nose and cove molding used to trim the table top is set a trifle below the top edge.

The decorative panels are covered with the desired patterned fabric or painting, using staples to fasten it around the perimeter. Then the panels are screwed to the base molding frame with 3/4-8 RH screws.

The table top is fastened with screws driven diagonally through the skirt pieces into pocket holes made as outlined earlier.

All of the nail holes are set and filled, and then the entire cabinet is sanded and finished as desired. The unit shown was finished in antique white, but other colors or stain may be used. When applying the finish, the decorative panels must be removed.

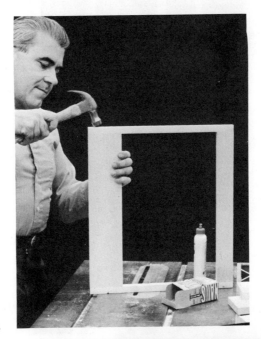

Fig. 7-98 The frame sections are assembled with nails and glue.

Fig. 7-99 The end base pieces are installed after the frame is partially assembled.

Fig. 7-100 To ensure accuracy, all sections must be carefully measured during assembly.

Fig. 7-101 Cove moldings are cut at the mounting angle. Tape is used to prevent shifting.

Fig. 7-102 Moldings are installed with brads and glue.

Materials List for Elegant Coffee Table

Part	Description	Size and Material	Quantity
1	Base, inner	3/4 × 3-3/4 × 17 pine	4
2	Base, outer	3/4 × 2 × 20 pine	4
3	Skirt	3/4 × 1-7/8 × 17 pine	4
4	Corner post	3/4 × 3/4 × 16-3/8 pine	4
5	Fabric support	1/2 × 9-3/4 × 16 plywood	4
6	Crown molding	1-1/2"	16'
7	Nose and cove molding	3/4"	8'
8	Base molding	1-1/2"	8'
9	Top	3/4 × 20-3/4 × 20-3/4 pine	1
10	Spline	1/4 × 3/4 × 2 plywood	4
A	Screw	1-1/4 – 8 RH	32
B	Finishing nails	2"	32

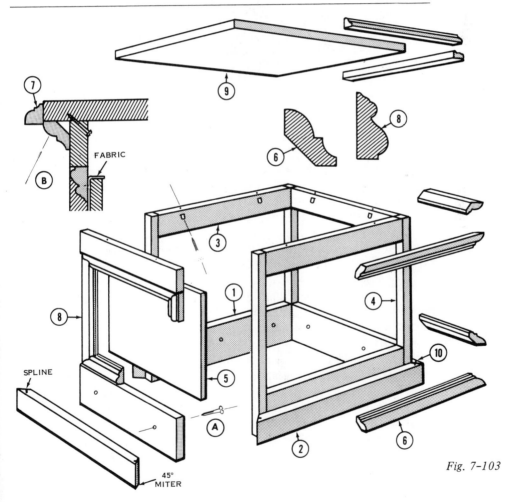

Fig. 7–103

Fig. 7-104

SUGAR BIN END TABLE

Somewhat modified for modern use, this sugar bin contains a roomy storage area, a large drawer made to look like three, and a substantial top suitable for a radio, lamp, or favorite accessory.

Except for the sides which are rabbeted to receive the back panel, all of the joints have been butted to simplify construction. The advanced worker may prefer to use dadoes for the three cabinet frames. This may easily be done by increasing the length of the frame pieces. The added length should equal twice the dado depth.

The parts are laid out and cut to size. Before assembling, the edges of the sides are rounded with a router. On the inner edges the rounding must stop at the area where the frame members are joined.

Cleats 5 and 6 are carefully located. When installed to the inner surface of the side panels, they serve as bearing surfaces for the skirt and door. The cleats are installed with 1-1/2-inch screws.

The frames are assembled with one dowel at each joint. Before assembling, the screw-mounting holes are bored as indicated. To prevent twisting, the ends are toenailed temporarily while clamping.

The door is made from glued-up stock with the annular rings reversed to prevent warping. If desired, cross-grain strips—which should be tongued-and-grooved, splined, or doweled—may be added to each end.

The skirt is fastened to the cabinet with two-inch screws driven from the back side of the lower cleat. The upper cleat serves as a door stop. When installing the base piece, washers are used under the screw heads to prevent the points from penetrating the front surface of the base.

The hinges used for the door are the non-mortise type with decorative finials. They are mounted to the top edge of the door 2-1/2 inches from each end. The other leaf of the hinge is fastened to the underside of the center frame.

The single drawer is made to look like three small drawers. (For instructions, see the drawer construction detail drawings.) The drawer is assembled with glue and 1-1/2-inch finishing nails. Instead of gluing the bottom panel, six annular-ring nails should be driven through the bottom into the rear panel.

Fig. 7-105 The frame members must be installed straight and square.

Fig. 7-106 A view from the underside shows how a nonmortise hinge is installed.

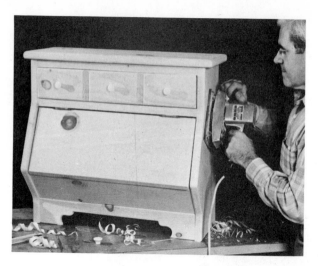

Fig. 7-107 Final sanding before applying the finish.

Materials List for Sugar Bin End Table

Part	Description	Size and Material	Quantity
1	Top	1-1/8 × 10-1/2 × 28-1/2 pine	1
2	Side	1-1/8 × 13-3/4 × 24 pine	2
3	Skirt	3/4 × 6-5/8 × 24-1/2 pine	1
4	Base	3/4 × 3-3/4 × 24-1/2 pine	1
5	Cleat (door)	3/4 × 1-1/2 × 10 pine	2
6	Cleat (skirt)	3/4 × 1-1/2 × 6-1/2 pine	2
7	Door	3/4 × 9-3/4 × 24-3/8 pine	1
8	Back	1/4 × 24 × 25 plywood	1
9	Frame end	1-1/8 × 1-3/4 × 6 pine	4
10	Frame front/rear	1-1/8 × 1-3/4 × 24-1/2 pine	6
11	Frame end, bottom	1-1/8 × 1-3/4 × 5 pine	2
12	Drawer front	3/4 × 4-3/8 × 24-1/4 pine	1
13	Drawer subfront	1/2 × 4-1/4 × 23-3/4 pine	1
14	Drawer side	1/2 × 4-1/4 × 9-1/8 pine	2
15	Drawer rear	1/2 × 3-3/4 × 23-3/4 pine	1
16	Drawer bottom	1/4 × 8-3/8 × 23-3/4 plywood	1
A	Dowel	3/8 × 2	12
B	Screw	2-1/2 – 10 RH	15
C	Screw	2 – 10 FH	14
D	Screw	1-1/2 – 8 FH	8
E	Nails	Finishing, 1-1/2"	34
F	Hinge	Nonmortise, 2"	2
G	Pull		3
H	Decorative eagle		1

Fig. 7-108 A slight overhang of the door at the lower edge eliminates the need for a handle.

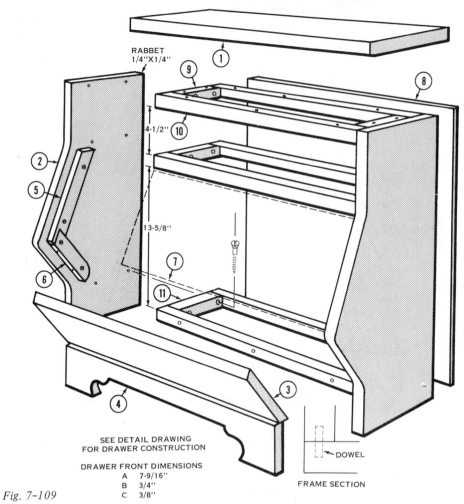

RABBET
1/4"X1/4"

4-1/2"

13-5/8"

DOWEL

FRAME SECTION

SEE DETAIL DRAWING
FOR DRAWER CONSTRUCTION

DRAWER FRONT DIMENSIONS
A   7-9/16"
B   3/4"
C   3/8"

Fig. 7-109

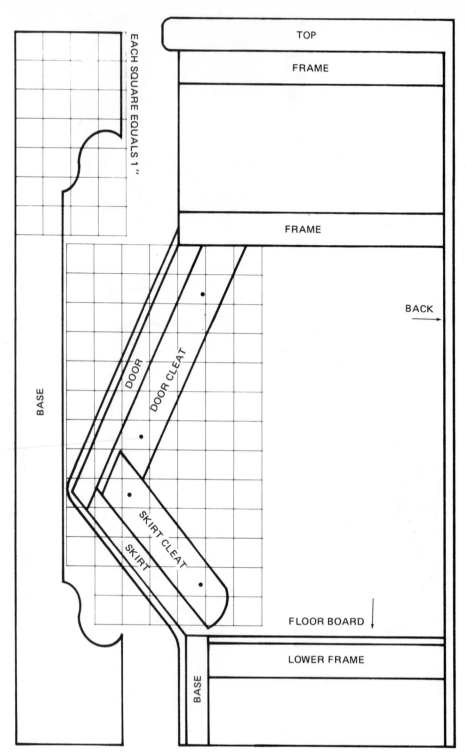

EACH SQUARE EQUALS 1"

TOP

FRAME

FRAME

BACK

DOOR

DOOR CLEAT

BASE

SKIRT CLEAT

SKIRT

FLOOR BOARD

LOWER FRAME

BASE

230

Fig. 7-110

CURIO CABINET/CLOCK

This well-proportioned curio cabinet displays favorite bric-a-brac and tells the time as well. Made of pine lumber and stock moldings, this project is easily made in an evening or two. Various clock movements, with or without chimes, are available for use in this cabinet. See the sources of supply section at the end of this chapter.

First, the side pieces are cut to size. Then the rabbet is made for the back panel, and the dadoes are cut for the shelves. The table saw may be used for cutting the dadoes, but because the boards are rather long, it is easier to use a router. The location of the dadoes (and rabbets) are marked carefully, and then the strips are clamped to the work to guide the router. To save time, both panels may be routed simultaneously. Since the depth of the cut is only one-fourth of an inch, it may be made in one pass without difficulty.

The curved shelf edge is then laid out on pattern paper which is cut with a knife and transferred to the shelves. A saber saw is used to cut the outline, and the edge is shaped with a router, using a beading or other suitable cutter.

Before doweling the apron and rails to the stiles, a one-sixteenth-inch rabbet is made at the rear outer edge of each stile as indicated in the sketch.

This rabbet serves as a break between the side panel and stile. After the front frame has been assembled, the router with a three-eighths-inch rounding cutter is used to break the edges within the dial and shelf area. When rounding the outer corners of the stiles, the rounding must be stopped at the points where the crown and nose moldings will be applied.

The front frame is installed with two-inch finishing nails and glue. The nails are placed only at the ends of the stiles and under the nose moldings where they will be concealed by the moldings. Likewise, two nails are driven through the upper and lower rails and through the apron and placed where they will be concealed by the moldings.

The moldings are cut and fit carefully, and the top closure is added. The dial is made to fit the top opening and is held in place with the five-inch cleats. Only screws—not glue—are used on the cleats so that the dial may be removed if necessary.

Fig. 7-111 The sharp edges of the side pieces are softened with sandpaper before installing the stiles.

Fig. 7-112 A router is used to shape the edges of the cabinet after assembly. A round or fancy cutter may be used.

Fig 7-113 The entire cabinet is smooth sanded before applying the moldings.

Fig. 7-114 The case takes shape when the moldings are added with brads and glue.

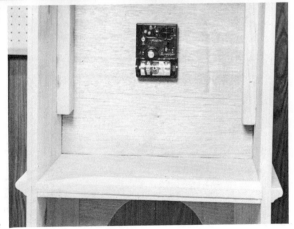

Fig. 7-115 An interior view shows how the dial board and movement are installed.

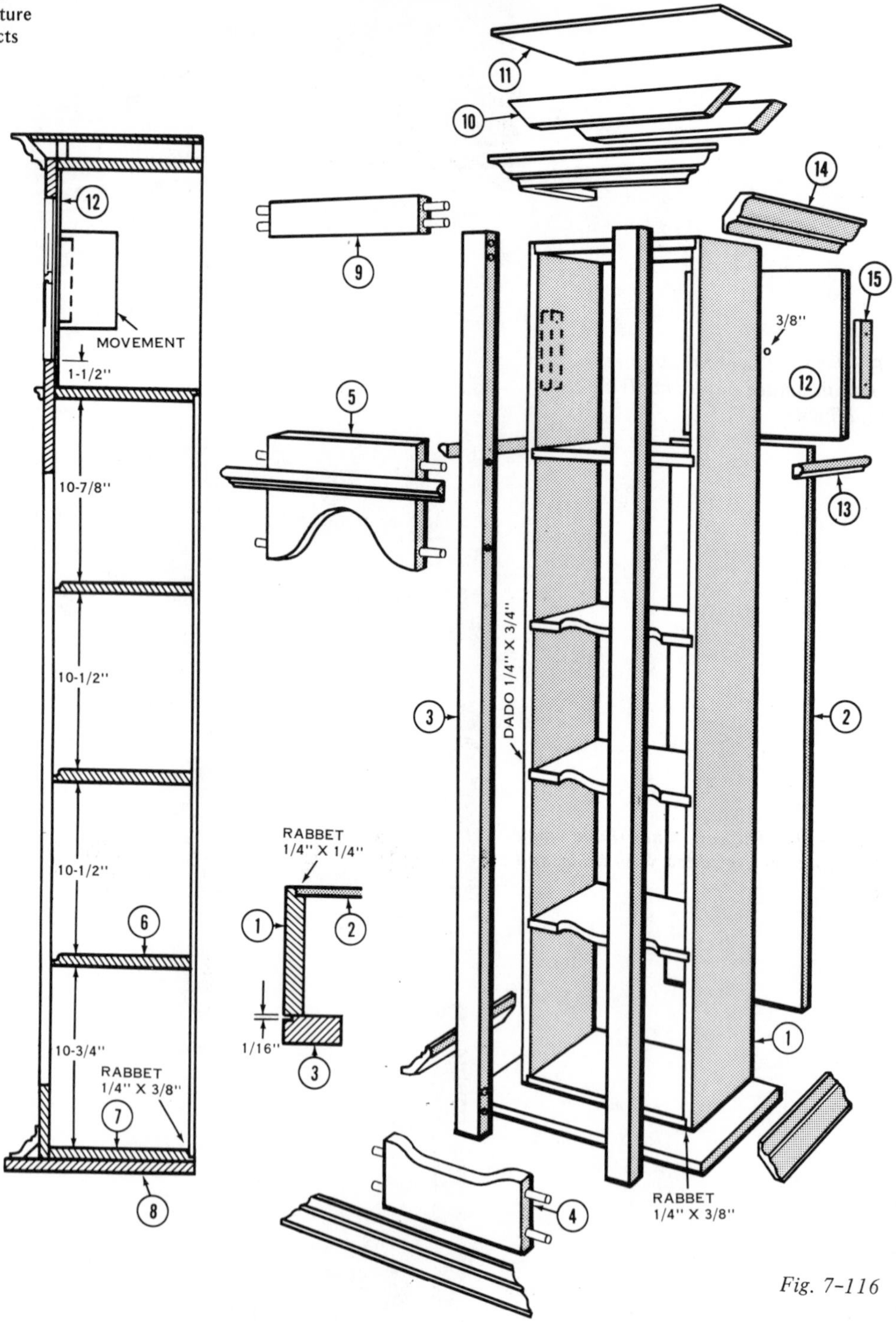

MOVEMENT

1-1/2''

10-7/8''

10-1/2''

10-1/2''

10-3/4''

RABBET
1/4'' X 3/8''

DADO 1/4'' X 3/4''

RABBET
1/4'' X 1/4''

1/16''

3/8''

RABBET
1/4'' X 3/8''

Fig. 7-116

Materials List for Curio Cabinet/Clock

Part	Description	Size and Material	Quantity
1	Side	1/2 X 9 X 60 pine	2
2	Back	1/4 X 12-3/8 X 45-3/4 plywood	1
3	Stile	3/4 X 1-5/8 X 60 pine	2
4	Lower rail	3/4 X 4-1/2 X 9-3/4 pine	1
5	Apron	3/4 X 7 X 9-3/4 pine	1
6	Shelf	3/4 X 8-3/4 X 12-1/2 pine	3
7	Top/bottom	3/4 X 9 X 12-1/2 pine	2
8	Base	3/4 X 11-5/8 X 16-3/8 pine	1
9	Top rail	3/4 X 2-3/8 X 9-3/4 pine	1
10	Closure support	3/4 X 1-3/16 X 14-1/2 pine	2
11	Top closure	1/8 X 10-1/2 X 14-1/2 hardboard	1
12	Dial board	1/4 X 11-7/8 X 12-7/8 plywood	1
13	Nose molding	5/8 X 3/4 X 4'	
14	Crown molding	2-1/2 X 8'	
15	Cleat	3/4 X 1 X 5 pine	2

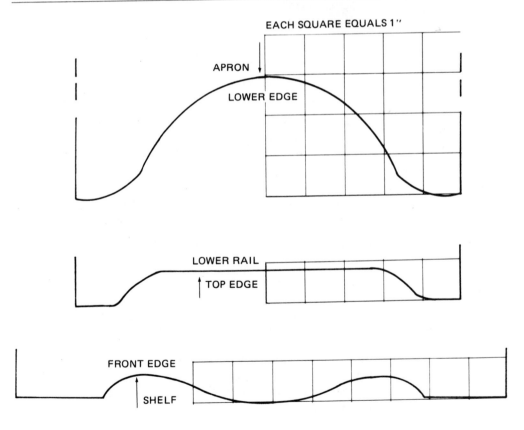

EACH SQUARE EQUALS 1"

APRON

LOWER EDGE

LOWER RAIL

TOP EDGE

FRONT EDGE

SHELF

Fig. 7-117

KNEEHOLE DESK

Plastic laminate and brass corners and pulls are combined in this attractive and functional kneehole desk. Made from less than a single sheet of plywood, it has seven roomy drawers, with the bottom two designed to hold letter-size file folders.

Inasmuch as the unit shown is covered with laminate, fir plywood is specified in the materials list. However, if a wood finish is desired, cabinet-grade lumber core plywood is suggested as an alternative. The edges should then be covered with veneer tape. Also, the top panel would require dadoes and rabbets to receive the four side pieces. The rabbets and dadoes should be 3/8 of an inch deep, and the side panels increased to 29-5/8 inches. It may also be advisable to allow the top to overhang the ends slightly, especially if tape is used for the edges.

The drawer compartments are built as two separate units. All of the dadoes are made three-sixteenths of an inch deep and three-quarters of an inch wide. Normally the dadoes would be made three-eighths of an inch deep, but because of the two sets—which are back to back—and the desire for uniformity, all are made the same. The back edge of the side pieces and the lower back edge of the top are rabbeted one-fourth of an inch by three-eighths of an inch to accept the back panel.

The frame members are cut from the remaining plywood and then assembled using two dowels at each joint. Because of the number of dowel holes needed, a doweling jig is recommended.

After the frames have been glued, the five-sixteenths-inch hardwood center guide is added to each. Glue and three-quarter-inch brads are used, and the strips are centered carefully since they guide the drawers.

Glue is applied, and the frames are fit into the side panels and screwed securely. The center frame is added last. Reinforcing cleats are temporarily installed front and back at the lower end of the kneehole opening. The cleats may be removed later after the top and back panels are installed. The back panel is then notched to clear the kneehole, and part of the rabbet at the upper part of the center dividers is cut away with a chisel.

The laminate should be applied as follows: first the end pieces, then the front, and finally the top. Strips for the front should be one inch wide.

The drawers are made with rabbeted and dadoed side members. Before assembling the pieces, the half-inch screw head clearance holes are bored in the subfront panel. The holes in the front panel are bored one-fourth of an inch in diameter and are in alignment with those of the subfront.

The size of the drawer front panel makes allowance for edge trimming with laminate. For non-laminate construction, one-eighth of an inch is added to the width and one-sixteenth of an inch to the height. The bottom edge is not laminated. The laminate is applied to the front panels in the following sequence: first the ends, then the top, and then the front of the drawer.

The drawer runners are cut to size and grooved 25/32 of an inch wide and 3/8 of an inch deep. The runners are centered carefully and installed temporarily with two brads, one at the front and one at the rear. In checking the drawers for fit, the runners should glide freely over the guide without binding, and the drawer front should center over the opening. Adjustments should be made if necessary, then the runners are installed permanently with glue and additional brads. Drawer tacks are added at the edge of the frames under the drawer sides to permit easy movement of the drawers.

Fig. 7-118 To ensure the frame members fit dadoes snugly, the fit should be checked.

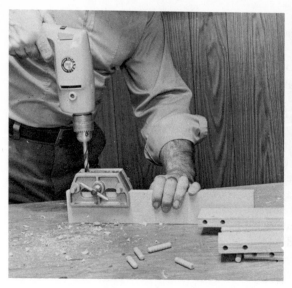

Fig. 7-119 A self-centering doweling jig is used to make dowel holes.

Fig. 7-120 Spiral grooved dowels are better than smooth ones.

Fig. 7-121 The frame members must be installed straight and square and checked as the work proceeds.

Fig. 7-122 The end sections are brought together when the center frame is installed.

Fig. 7-123 *The overhang of the top panel is marked and cut to assure accuracy.*

SEE DETAIL DRAWING
FOR DRAWER CONSTRUCTION

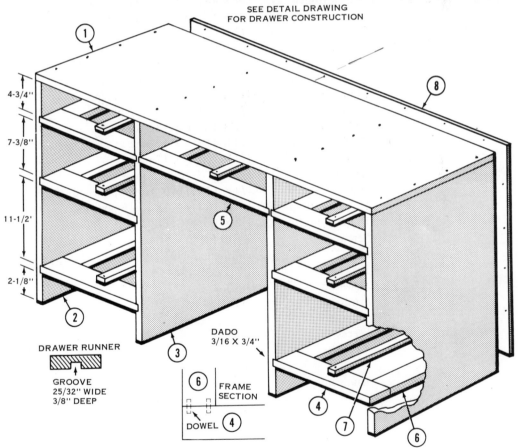

4-3/4"

7-3/8"

11-1/2'

2-1/8"

DRAWER RUNNER

GROOVE
25/32" WIDE
3/8" DEEP

DADO
3/16 X 3/4"

FRAME
SECTION

DOWEL

Fig. 7-124

239

Materials List for Kneehole Desk

Part	Description	Size and Material	Quantity
1	Top	3/4 × 18 × 49-1/2 plywood	1
2	End	3/4 × 18 × 29-1/4 plywood	2
3	Divider	3/4 × 18 × 29-1/4 plywood	2
4	Frame, Front/rear	3/4 × 2-1/2 × 13-7/8 plywood	12
5	Frame, Front/rear	3/4 × 2-1/2 × 19-7/8 plywood	2
6	Frame side	3/4 × 2-1/2 × 12-3/4 plywood	14
7	Drawer guide	5/16 × 3/4 × 16-1/2 oak	7
8	Back	1/4 × 29-5/8 × 48-3/4 plywood	1
9	Drawer front	3/4 × 4-9/16 × 13-5/16 plywood	2
10	Drawer front	3/4 × 7-3/16 × 13-5/16 plywood	2
11	Drawer front	3/4 × 11-5/16 × 13-5/16 plywood	2
12	Drawer front	3/4 × 4-9/16 × 19-5/16 plywood	1
13	Drawer subfront	1/2 × 4-9/16 × 12-5/16 pine	2
14	Drawer back	1/2 × 4-1/16 × 12-5/16 pine	2
15	Drawer subfront	1/2 × 7-3/16 × 12-5/16 pine	2
16	Drawer back	1/2 × 6-11/16 × 12-5/16 pine	2
17	Drawer subfront	1/2 × 11-5/16 × 12-5/16 pine	2
18	Drawer back	1/2 × 10-13/16 × 12-5/16 pine	2
19	Drawer subfront	1/2 × 4-9/16 × 18-5/16 pine	1
20	Drawer back	1/2 × 4-1/16 × 18-5/16 pine	1
21	Drawer side	1/2 × 4-9/16 × 17 pine	6
22	Drawer side	1/2 × 7-3/16 × 17 pine	4
23	Drawer side	1/2 × 11-5/16 × 17 pine	4
24	Drawer bottom	1/4 × 12-13/16 × 16-1/4 plywood	6
25	Drawer bottom	1/4 × 16-1/4 × 18-13/16 plywood	1
26	Drawer runner	1/2 × 1-3/4 × 16-1/2 oak	7
A	Screw	3 – 10 FH	28
B	Nail	Finishing, 1-1/2"	14
C	Brad	1 × 18	24
D	Dowel	3/8 × 2	56
E	Hardware	Brass	
	Corners		2
	Tees		12
	Crosses		2
	Pulls		7
F	Laminate		30 sq. ft.

Fig. 7-125

EARLY AMERICAN CHEST

Although this chest of drawers looks complicated to build, it is not. Except for the brads used to fasten the moldings, all of the screws are concealed. The moldings are stock items, available where the lumber is purchased.

The top and side sections must be made with glued-up stock, unless plywood is used. If the sections must be glued the annular rings should be alternated to prevent warping. Also, if gluing is necessary, the width should be made a trifle wider than the finished size to eliminate the need for cauls under the clamps. Dowels or splines are used for strength.

After the sides are cut and trimmed, the sawn edge is dressed with a plane or jointer, then the quarter-inch by three-eighths-inch rabbet is cut at the back edge of each side piece.

Flat, knot-free stock should be selected for the stiles and rails and then ripped to size and cut to the required length. The rails must be uniform in length. When drilling the dowel holes, they are checked for alignment. A doweling jig or dowel centers may be used to locate the holes accurately. The dowel holes are bored 1-1/16 inches deep, then the parts are assembled and clamped securely to make up the front frame.

The top and rear frames are constructed next. The rear frame consists of two crosspieces connected to the vertical member and is assembled with dowels. The vertical piece will support the drawer slide hardware. In assembly, the back edge of the rear assembly must line up with the rear edge of the rabbets cut in the side pieces.

The rear section and front frame are attached to the sides with glue and two-inch finishing nails. For better construction, the front frame may be splined or doweled to the sides. After the glue sets, all joints are planed or scraped flush.

The base pieces are cut to size and before assembling are checked for proper fit against the cabinet. The four half-inch diameter button holes in the front base piece are placed three-quarters of an inch from the edge to enhance the appearance. The holes would be too close to the edge if bored in the normal manner. The screws are simply driven at an angle into the base side pieces. The filler strips at the base are used to add thickness to the base pieces. These are concealed by the bed moldings. When mitering, the moldings should be held at the mounting angle and then installed with glue and brads.

Fig. 7-126 Adequate pressure must be used when clamping the frame. Overtightening must be avoided.

Fig. 7-127 If properly cut and glued, the frame should square up.

Nose and cove moldings are added to the ends and front edge of the top. Before installing the top, the cleats are added to the top section, driving two-inch roundhead screws from the inner edges. Also before installing the top, the backboard and end pieces are made. These are shaped with a rounding cutter; then the groove is cut and the backboard carved. These are fastened from the underside of the top. Then the top is mounted, with the screws driven from the underside of the cleats. Next, the molding is added to the underside of the top.

The drawers are made to operate with center-slide hardware. For installation procedure, the manufacturer's recommendations should be followed.

Fig. 7-128 The base fastens to a filler strip, thus forming the necessary shoulder for the bed molding.

Fig. 7-129 Carving the floral design with a grinding tool fitted with a burr cutter.

Fig. 7-130 The completed cabinet with the center slide-drawer hardware installed.

Fig. 7-131 The fit of the drawer
should be checked to ensure it closes
properly.

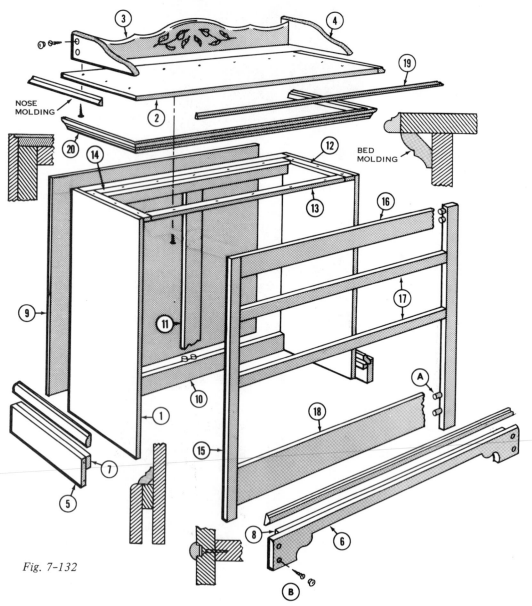

NOSE
MOLDING

BED
MOLDING

Fig. 7-132

Materials List for Early American Chest

Part	Description	Size and Material	Quantity
1	Side	3/4 × 15-3/8 × 34 pine	2
2	Top	3/4 × 17-1/4 × 36 pine	1
3	Backboard	3/4 × 4-1/4 × 33-1/2 pine	1
4	End	3/4 × 3 × 13 pine	2
5	Base end	3/4 × 4 × 16-7/8 pine	2
6	Base front	3/4 × 4 × 36-5/8 pine	1
7	Filler, end	3/4 × 1-1/2 × 16-7/8 pine	2
8	Filler, front	3/4 × 1-1/2 × 33-5/8 pine	1
9	Back	1/4 × 32-7/8 × 34 plywood	1
10	Crosspiece	3/4 × 2-3/4 × 32-1/8 pine	2
11	Drawer support	3/4 × 2-3/4 × 28-1/2 pine	1
12	Frame end	3/4 × 1-3/8 × 14-1/4 pine	2
13	Frame front	3/4 × 1-3/8 × 29-3/8 pine	1
14	Frame rear	3/4 × 1-3/8 × 29-3/8 pine	1
15	Stile	3/4 × 1-7/16 × 34 pine	2
16	Top rail	3/4 × 2-3/4 × 30-3/4 pine	2
17	Intermediate rail	3/4 × 1-7/16 × 30-3/4 pine	2
18	Bottom rail	3/4 × 4-3/8 × 30-3/4 pine	1
19	Nose molding	3/4″ × 8′	
20	Bed molding	3/4″ × 16′	
21	Drawer front	3/4 × 4-3/4 × 31-1/2 pine	1
22	Drawer subfront	1/2 × 3-5/8 × 30 pine	1
23	Drawer side	1/2 × 3-5/8 × 14 pine	1
24	Drawer rear	1/2 × 3-1/8 × 30 pine	1
25	Drawer bottom	1/4 × 13-1/4 × 30 plywood	3
26	Drawer front	3/4 × 8 × 31-1/2 pine	1
27	Drawer subfront	1/2 × 6-7/8 × 30 pine	1
28	Drawer side	1/2 × 7-7/8 × 14 pine	1
29	Drawer rear	1/2 × 6-3/8 × 30 pine	1
30	Drawer front	3/4 × 10-7/8 × 31-1/2 pine	1
31	Drawer subfront	1/2 × 9-3/4 × 30 pine	1
32	Drawer side	1/2 × 9-3/4 × 14 pine	1
33	Drawer rear	1/2 × 9-1/4 × 30 pine	1
A	Dowel	3/8 × 2	22
B	Screw	1-1/2 – 8 FH – 5/8″ buttons	8
C	Screw	2 – 10 RH	14
D	Screw	1-1/4 – 8 FH	48
E	Nail	Finishing, 2″	24
F	Nail	Finishing, 1-1/2″	48
G	Brad	1 × 18	48

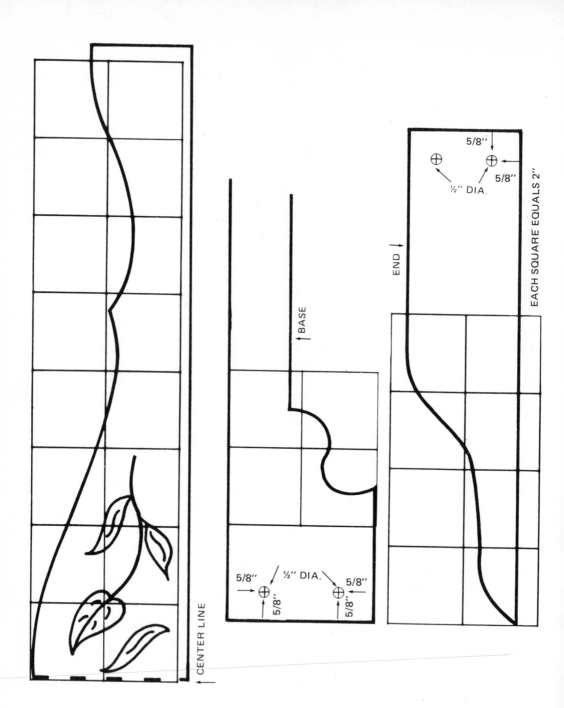

CENTER LINE

BASE

½" DIA.

5/8"

5/8"

5/8"

5/8"

END

5/8"

5/8"

½" DIA.

EACH SQUARE EQUALS 2"

246

SOURCES OF SUPPLY

Adjustable Clamp Co. 417 No. Ashland Ave. Chicago, Ill. 60622	Clamps
Amerock Corp. Rockford, Ill. 61101	Cabinet hardware
Armor Products Box 290 Deer Park, N.Y. 11729	Specialty cabinet hardware, Clock components and dials
Binks Manufacturing Co. 9205 W. Belmont Ave. Franklin Park, Ill. 60131	Spraying equipment
The Black & Decker Manufacturing Co. Towson, Md. 21204	Power and hand tools
Brookstone Company 127 Vise Farm Rd. Peterborough, N.H. 03458	Small tools and hardware
Industrial Finishing Products 465 Logan St. Brooklyn, N.Y. 11208	Finishing materials
Rockwell International 400 No. Lexington Ave. Pittsburgh, Pa. 15208	Power and hand tools
Sears, Roebuck & Co. Chicago, Ill. 60607	Power and hand tools, Hardware, spray equipment
Wetzler Clamp Co., Inc. 11th St. and 43rd Ave. Long Island City, N.Y. 11101	Clamps

INDEX